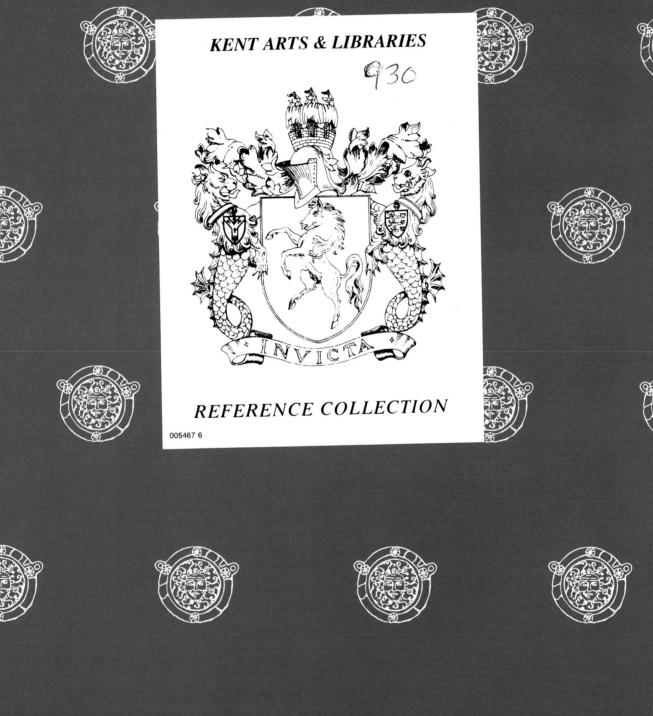

HOW *WOULD* YOU SURVIVE AS AN

ANCIENT ROMAN?

Written by
Anita Ganeri

Illustrated by
John James

Created & Designed by
David Salariya

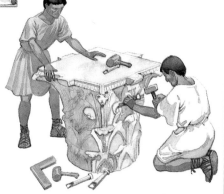

WATTS BOOKS

LONDON • NEW YORK • SYDNEY

David Salariya *Director*
Penny Clarke *Editor*
Dr. Stephen Johnson *Consultant*

ANITA GANERI
was born in India. She holds a master's degree from the University of Cambridge in French, German and Indian studies. She has written over 50 books for children, on a wide range of subjects including history and natural history. She lives in Ilkely, West Yorkshire.

JOHN JAMES
studied illustration at Eastbourne College of Art. Since leaving art school in 1983, he has specialized in historical reconstructions and architectural cross-sections. He is a major contributor to the *Timelines* and *X-Ray Picture Book* Series. John James lives in East Sussex with his wife and daughters.

DAVID SALARIYA
was born in Dundee, Scotland, where he studied illustration and printmaking. He has illustrated a wide range of books on botanical, historical and mythical subjects. He has created and designed many new series of books for publishers in the UK and overseas. In 1989 he established The Salariya Book Company. He lives in Brighton with his wife, the illustrator Shirley Willis.

Printed in Belgium

A CIP catalogue record for this book is available from the British Library.
First published in 1994 by WATTS BOOKS
This edition 1997

STEPHEN JOHNSON
studied Classics and Archaeology at Oxford University, concentrating on Roman fortifications. He has written several books on Roman forts, and on Roman Britain, including one on Hadrian's Wall. Since 1984 he has worked for English Heritage as an Archaeologist, Publisher, and most recently as a Regional Director.

WATTS BOOKS
96 Leonard Street
London EC2A 4RH
ISBN 0-7496-1251-7
Dewey Decimal Classification Number 937

CONTENTS

BECOMING AN ANCIENT ROMAN . . .

4   <u>Time Spiral</u>
Back to the Age of the Ancient Romans

6   Basic Facts about Roman Life

8   Your Map of the Roman World

10   Begin Your New Life Here

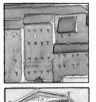

14   **<u>YOUR HOUSE</u>**
WHAT WOULD IT BE LIKE?

16   **<u>CITY OR COUNTRY?</u>**
WHAT WOULD YOUR LIFE BE LIKE?

18   **<u>YOUR FAMILY</u>**
WHAT WOULD YOURS BE LIKE?

20   **<u>FOOD AND DRINK</u>**
WHAT WOULD YOU EAT AND DRINK?

22   **<u>YOUR CLOTHES</u>**
WHAT WOULD YOU WEAR?

24   **<u>SICKNESS AND HEALTH</u>**
HOW WOULD YOU KEEP CLEAN AND HEALTHY?

26   **<u>EDUCATION</u>**
WHAT WOULD YOU LEARN?

28   **<u>CAREERS</u>**
WHAT WORK WOULD YOU DO?

30   **<u>ENTERTAINMENT</u>**
HOW WOULD YOU HAVE FUN?

32   **<u>LAW AND ORDER</u>**
WOULD YOU OBEY THE LAW?

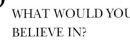

34   **<u>TRAVEL AND TRADE</u>**
WHERE WOULD YOU GO?

36   **<u>THE ARMY</u>**
WHAT WOULD A SOLDIER'S LIFE BE LIKE?

38   **<u>THE GODS</u>**
WHAT WOULD YOU BELIEVE IN?

40   **<u>BIRTH, MARRIAGE AND DEATH</u>**
WHAT HAPPENS WHEN YOU ARE BORN, GET MARRIED OR DIE?

42   How Do We Know?

44   Ancient Roman Timespan

46   Have You Survived?

47   Glossary

48   Index

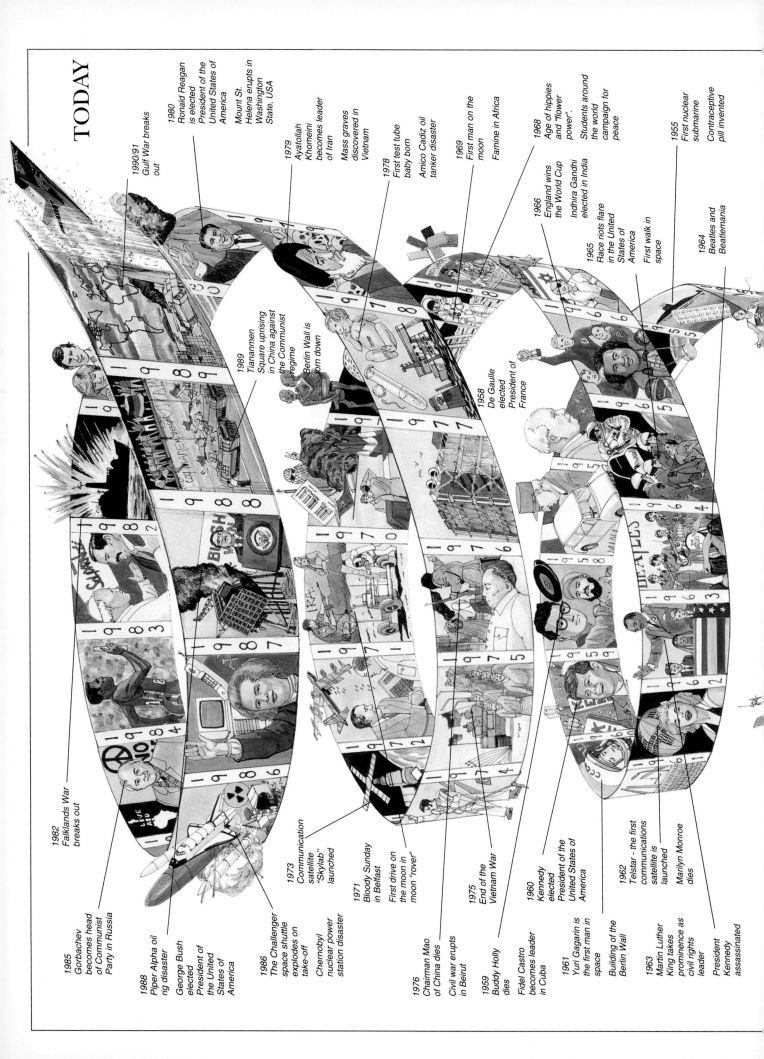

TODAY

1990/91 Gulf War breaks out

1980 Ronald Reagan is elected President of the United States of America

Mount St. Helena erupts in Washington State, USA

1979 Ayatollah Khomeini becomes leader of Iran

Mass graves discovered in Vietnam

1978 First test tube baby born

Amico Cadiz oil tanker disaster

1969 First man on the moon

Famine in Africa

1968 Age of hippies and "flower power".

Students around the world campaign for peace

1966 England wins the World Cup

Indhira Gandhi elected in India

1965 Race riots flare in the United States of America

First walk in space

1955 First nuclear submarine

Contraceptive pill invented

1964 Beatles and Beatlemania

1989 Tiananmen Square uprising in China against the Communist regime

Berlin Wall is torn down

1958 De Gaulle elected President of France

1982 Falklands War breaks out

1973 Communication satellite "Skylab" launched

1971 Bloody Sunday in Belfast

First drive on the moon "rover"

1975 End of the Vietnam War

1960 Kennedy elected President of the United States of America

1962 Telstar - the first communications satellite is launched

Marilyn Monroe dies

1985 Gorbachev becomes head of Communist Party in Russia

1988 Piper Alpha oil rig disaster

George Bush elected President of the United States of America

1986 The Challenger space shuttle explodes on take-off

Chernobyl nuclear power station disaster

1976 Chairman Mao of China dies

Civil war erupts in Beirut

1959 Buddy Holly dies

Fidel Castro becomes leader in Cuba

1961 Yuri Gagarin is the first man in space

Building of the Berlin Wall

1963 Martin Luther King takes prominence as civil rights leader

President Kennedy assassinated

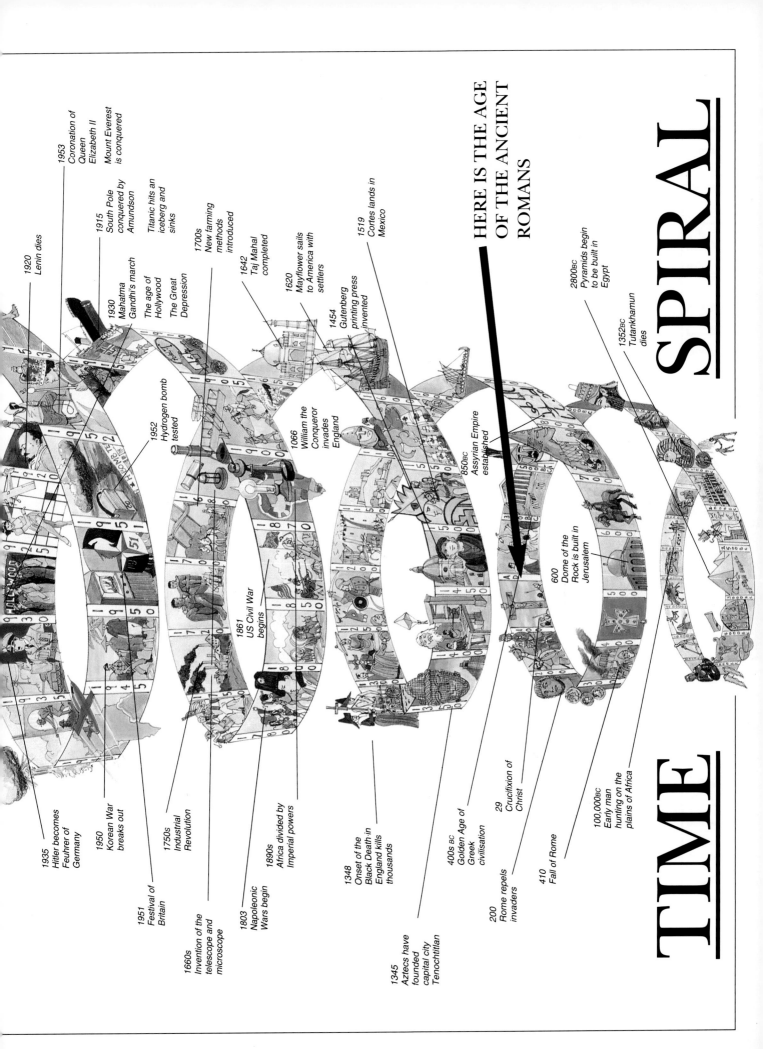

SPIRAL

TIME

HERE IS THE AGE
OF THE ANCIENT
ROMANS

1953
Coronation of
Queen
Elizabeth II

Mount Everest
is conquered

1920
Lenin dies

1915
South Pole
conquered by
Amundson

Titanic hits an
iceberg and
sinks

1930
Mahatma
Gandhi's march

The age of
Hollywood

1700s
New farming
methods
introduced

The Great
Depression

1642
Taj Mahal
completed

1620
Mayflower sails
to America with
settlers

1454
Gutenberg
printing press
invented

1519
Cortes lands in
Mexico

2800BC
Pyramids begin
to be built in
Egypt

1352BC
Tutankhamun
dies

1952
Hydrogen bomb
tested

1066
William the
Conqueror
invades
England

850BC
Assyrian Empire
established

600
Dome of the
Rock is built in
Jerusalem

1861
US Civil War
begins

1935
Hitler becomes
Feuhrer of
Germany

1950
Korean War
breaks out

1951
Festival of
Britain

1750s
Industrial
Revolution

1660s
Invention of the
telescope and
microscope

1803
Napoleonic
Wars begin

1890s
Africa divided by
Imperial powers

1348
Onset of the
Black Death in
England kills
thousands

400s BC
Golden Age of
Greek
civilisation

29
Crucifixion of
Christ

200
Rome repels
invaders

410
Fall of Rome

100,000BC
Early man
hunting on the
plains of Africa

1345
Aztecs have
founded
capital city
Tenochtitlan

The Republic

YOU ARRIVED in Rome when it was the centre of a powerful Empire, but the story of Rome begins much earlier. The villages beside the river Tiber became a powerful city, conquering the rest of Italy and the lands around the Mediterranean Sea. This period, from 510-27 BC, is called the Roman Republic and Rome was governed by the Senate, which represented the people of the city. In 44 BC, Julius Caesar, Rome's leader, was assassinated in the Senate by his rivals.

The Roman Empire

IN 27 BC, after many years of civil war, Caesar's adopted son, Augustus, seized power. He became Emperor, the ruler in charge of Rome and the lands it controlled. Augustus was a wise and just leader. When he died in AD 14, he was made a god and a temple was erected in his honour. Not all the Emperors who followed him used their power so well. Your travels have brought you to Rome during the early years of the Empire. The city is full of new buildings, reflecting its wealth and power.

Roman Beliefs

THE ROMANS looked to their gods for protection and tried to gain their favour with offerings, sacrifices and festivals. Grand temples were built for the official gods of the state; ordinary families worshipped their own gods at home. Romans were also superstitious. They often consulted a soothsayer or a fortune teller before an important occasion. Many of the Romans' official gods were similar to the Greeks'. The Romans' Jupiter was very like the Greeks' Zeus.

The Army

THE ROMAN ARMY was a huge well-drilled, well-disciplined, highly successful military machine. Without it there could have been no Roman Empire. The army also offered a good career to young recruits, with decent pay and conditions and a chance to see more of the Empire. The only snag was that you had to join up for twenty-five years. Roman citizens joined as legionaries; non-citizens as auxiliaries. Young noblemen often joined up as the first step in a political career.

Clothes & Status

THE CLOTHES people wore showed their rank in society – Romans were very status conscious. Boys under 14 (if they were citizens' sons) wore a toga with a purple stripe (the *toga praetexta*). At 14 they wore the pure white toga (the *toga virilis*). Senators (members of the Senate) also wore the *toga praetexta*. The emperor's toga was purple. Wealthy women wore a long robe over a tunic, with a shawl, called a *palla*, draped over their head and shoulders.

Travel & Trade

ROME WAS THE centre of a huge Empire. The rest of Italy counted as a province of the Empire, even though Rome stood in its midst. The excellent road system and the peace and safety of the times, known as the *Pax Romana*, encouraged more people to travel and trade abroad. Archaeological evidence shows the Romans traded all round the Mediterranean. They took Roman customs and culture with them, and also adopted new ideas, such as Christianity from the east.

Rich & Poor

YOUR LIFE in ancient Rome will greatly depend on whether your family is rich or poor. There are far more poor families than rich ones, and the contrasts between them are very great. Rich Romans led pleasant lives, with lovely homes, good food, fine clothes and plenty of slaves to wait on them. If you were poor, however, you had to work hard for your living, scrimp and save some money, and do everything for yourself. Yours was certainly no life of leisure.

City & Country

MANY ROMANS lived in large, crowded cities throughout the Empire. The great majority, however, lived and worked in the countryside, mostly as poor farmers. Others worked on the estates of rich landowners, who lived in the cities and visited their estates occasionally. The main crops were olives for oil, grapes for wine and grain for bread – the staple ingredients of the Roman diet. The population of Rome was growing so fast that grain had to be imported, much of it from Egypt.

Slaves

WITHOUT SLAVES the Roman Empire would have ground to a halt. They did all the hardest and dirtiest work, as well as waiting on the wealthy. Most were prisoners of war. Greek slaves were often well educated and so were highly prized as teachers and doctors. Some slaves were well treated and eventually given their freedom. Others became very influential, as secretaries to senators or even Emperors. The vast majority of them, however, led miserable lives.

Language

MANY DIFFERENT languages were spoken throughout the Roman Empire, but the official language was Latin. This was important in bringing some unity to the various parts of the Empire. Educated Romans also learnt Greek. Latin is still studied today, and is also the official language of the Roman Catholic Church. Here are a few words to start you off – *Salve!* (Hello) and *Vale!* (Goodbye). *O me miserum!* (Woe is me) is a useful phrase if things get you down!

Letters & Numerals

MOST EUROPEAN languages still use the basic Latin alphabet. The alphabet used by the Romans had twenty-two letters. There was no W or Y, I and J were written as I, and U and V were written as V. Roman numerals, however, are rarely used now. They are the letters I = 1, V = 5, X = 10, L = 50, C = 100, D = 500 and M = 1000. These are combined in different ways to make all other numbers. For example: IX = 9, but XI = 11, LX = 60, but XL = 40 and XVII – V = XII.

Names

NOW THAT YOU KNOW so much about ancient Rome, it is time to begin your journey. First, however, you need a name. Like us, many Romans had two names, a personal name and their family name. Some Roman personal names may be familiar to you already; many are still in use. Here are a few to choose from: for girls, Julia, Livia, Drusilla, Antonia or Claudia; for boys, Marcus, Julius, Antonius, Titus, Caius, Didius, Marius or Septimus. Take your pick and off you go.

YOUR MAP OF THE ROMAN WORLD

YOU HAVE ARRIVED in the city of Rome sometime in the 1st century AD, during the time of the Roman Empire. This period of Rome's history began in 27 BC when Augustus seized power and became the first Emperor. By this time, Rome was already a superpower and master of the lands around the Mediterranean Sea, known to the Romans as *Mare Nostrum* – 'Our Sea'. Under Augustus, the Roman Empire expanded as more overseas territories, called provinces, were added.

The map opposite shows the Roman Empire at its greatest size, under Emperor Trajan (AD 98-117). He added the province of Dacia (modern Rumania) and land in the Middle East. At its height, the Roman Empire covered about 30 of today's countries and had some 50 million people living within its borders. Trajan's successor, Hadrian, thought the Empire was getting too big and out of control. He stopped the expansion and tried to consolidate and fortify Roman lands.

THE MAP (above) shows the territories which made up the Roman Empire. It was huge, stretching from Britain in the west to Syria in the east, and from Germany in the north to Tunisia in the south.

Celtic farmer

Londi

Aqueduct

Tarragona

HISPANIA

Cordoba

Date palms

THE CITY OF ROME itself is the base for your expedition. Many of the places mentioned in this book are in Rome. This was the capital of the Empire, the biggest, grandest and busiest city in the Roman world. It had grown from tiny settlements dating from around 800 BC. In AD 64, during Nero's reign, the city was devastated by fire. It was rebuilt and enlarged, but it was not until AD 271 that a strong defensive wall was built. This was called the Aurelian Wall.

BEFORE SETTING off on your adventures you make a sacrifice to the gods. Any Roman would do the same, because it is always best to have the gods on your side!

Northern horsemen

Attacking the Empire's frontiers

Grain

Prisoners of war

Skins

GERMANIA

Defending the Empire's frontiers

GAUL

Military fort

DACIA

Ravenna

Amphora

BLACK   SEA

ITALY

Senator

Constantinople

Marseilles

Rome

Bridge

Naples

Pergamum

GREECE

Smyrna

MEDITERRANEAN SEA

Athens

Ephesus

SICILY

Corinth

Antioch

Carthage

CRETE

CYPRUS

Damascus

Temple

Trading ship

Jerusalem

Lepcis Magna

Cyrene

Alexandria

AFRICA

Pyramids

EGYPT

Market building

Roman colonist

Shadoof for raising water

BEGIN YOUR NEW LIFE HERE

HERE AND ON the next two pages is a panorama of the world of ancient Rome which awaits you. It is not meant to be a true-to-life picture, for you would not usually find all these things happening so close together. It is simply to act as your guide to this book. Start wherever you wish and follow the Q options.

YOU CAN hear the roar of the crowd at the Circus all over Rome. What are they watching? *Go to page 31*

ROMAN CITIES are famous for their excellent water supplies. How does water reach a city? *Go to page 16*

WHAT do you expect to eat and drink in ancient Rome? What might be carried in these jars? *Go to pages 20-21*

THE ROMANS worship many gods and goddesses. Which are the most important in their lives?
Go to pages 38-39

THE ROMANS like nothing better than a good gladiator fight. What types of gladiators might you see?
Go to page 31

ROME is built along the banks of the river Tiber. Who founded the city, according to the legend?
Go to page 16

MERCHANT SHIPS from all over the world come to Ostia, the port near Rome, to unload. What cargoes do they carry?
Go to pages 34-35

ROADS have been built all over the Roman Empire. How and why were they built?
Go to page 34

THE ROMAN army is the power behind the Empire. What sort of life does a legionary lead?
Go to pages 36-37

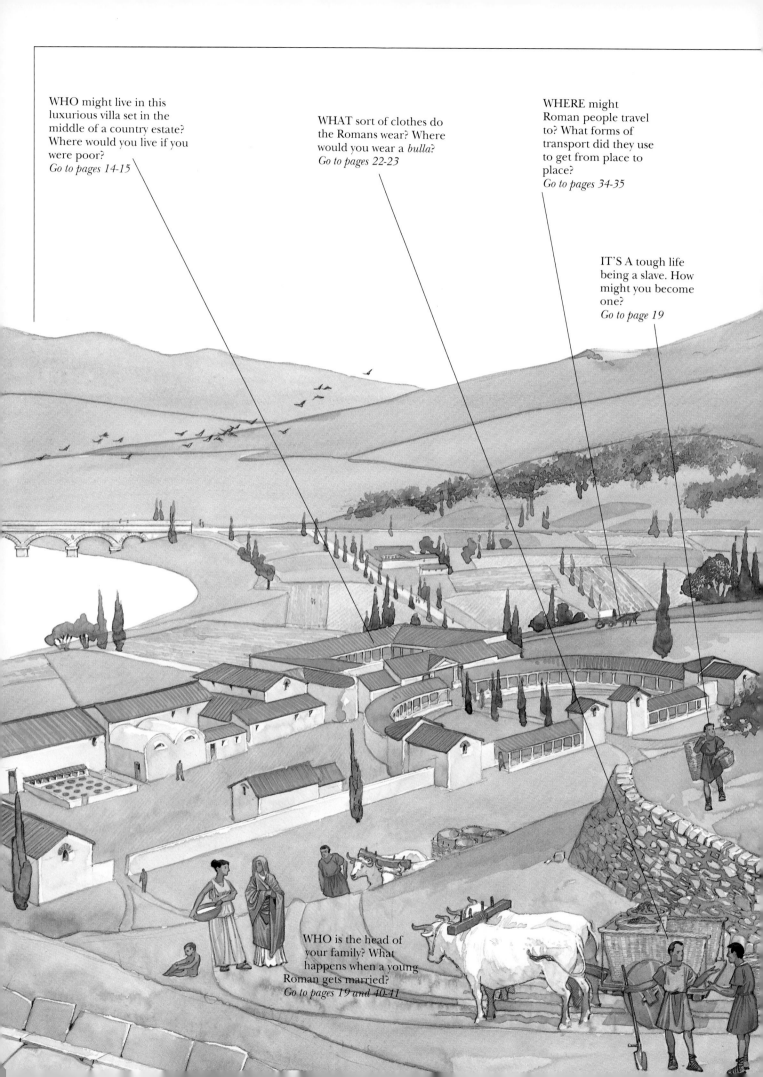

WHO might live in this luxurious villa set in the middle of a country estate? Where would you live if you were poor?
Go to pages 14-15

WHAT sort of clothes do the Romans wear? Where would you wear a *bulla*?
Go to pages 22-23

WHERE might Roman people travel to? What forms of transport did they use to get from place to place?
Go to pages 34-35

IT'S A tough life being a slave. How might you become one?
Go to page 19

WHO is the head of your family? What happens when a young Roman gets married?
Go to pages 19 and 40-41

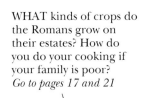

WHAT kinds of crops do the Romans grow on their estates? How do you do your cooking if your family is poor?
Go to pages 17 and 21

WHO makes the laws in Rome? What might happen if you break the law?
Go to pages 32-33

YOUR HOUSE
WHAT WOULD IT BE LIKE?

The walls of a new villa are built of rubble, bound together with limestone and clay.

The corners of the villa walls are shaped and constructed from layers of brick and stone.

A mixture of flat tiles (tegulae) and ridge-shaped tiles (imbrices) cover the roof of the villa.

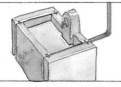
The villa has its own water supply and drainage system, with terracotta pipes draining into a cistern.

THE SORT OF HOUSE you lived in depended very much on whether your family was rich or poor. In a big city like Rome, poor people lived in cramped, dingy, high-rise blocks of flats. In general the higher the storey on which you lived, the smaller and pokier the flat. Because living space was in short supply in Rome, blocks of flats were built higher and higher to cram more people in – and make the landlords richer! Eventually they became so unsafe that a law was passed limiting them to four or five storeys. They were also terrible fire hazards. The upper storeys were normally built of wood. As cooking and heating were done with charcoal braziers, sparks could easily set material or wooden furniture alight. Some flats were much more luxurious, with larger, lighter rooms. They were usually on the lower floors and cost more to live in, so only the well-off could afford them.

Flat roof

Central courtyard

Shops

(Above) THE GROUND FLOOR of this block of flats in Ostia, near Rome, is let as shops and taverns. Stairs lead up to the flats. There's a constant stream of people on the stairs, fetching food and water or just gossiping.

(Below) THE HOUSE OF MENANDER in Pompeii bustled with activity, as befitted the town house of an important Roman family. Slaves cooked and cleaned, and carried out their master's or mistress's every wish. Clients (people seeking favours) sat patiently on benches around the *atrium*, waiting to see their patron, the head of the family.

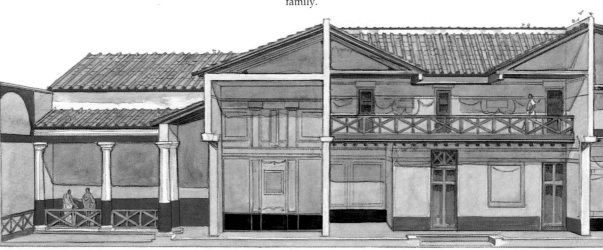

Q

There is to be a great feast in the villa in a few days' time. How do you make the fish sauce?

Go to page 21

LAYING A MOSAIC

Some of the villa's floors are decorated with intricate mosaics.

Mosaics are pictures made of small pieces of stone or glass.

First, an expert mosaic maker draws a plan of the design and pattern.

A small area of the floor at a time is covered in a layer of wet plaster.

Then the pieces of stone are laid, according to the expert's design.

The mosaic is smoothed off and polished. A good job has been done!

Summer dining-room

The floors and walls of the villa are decorated in elaborate mosaics and frescoes but there is not as much furniture as we are used to today. Couches are used for dining or sleeping. Household objects are stored in wooden chests; valuables are locked in metal strongboxes to deter thieves. Many of the tables are portable so they can be used wherever they are needed. Olive oil lamps provide light in the evening.

Bathhouse
Bakehouse

Wine pressing room

Main courtyard

Temple

Forecourt of villa

CENTRAL HEATING

It's warm in Rome but in colder parts of the Empire, villas have underfloor heating systems.

Warm air from the basement fires flows between the brick or concrete columns which support the ground floor.

Then the warm air flows through wall ducts into the rooms of the villa and quickly heats them.

The fires are in the basement of the villa. They are kept well stoked by the household slaves.

Wine storage yard

Storage barn

Pigsties

Overseer's quarters

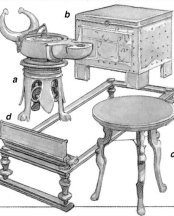

(**Left**) Roman furniture: *a.* lamp; *b.* storage chest; *c.* lamp stand; *d.* couch frame.

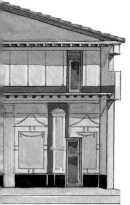

If your family were very wealthy, you probably had a *domus* (a house in town) and a country *villa*, on your father's estate. In the country you and your family lived in the main house, built around an airy central courtyard (*atrium*). On a hot summer's day, you could relax by the pool in the large, shady garden. The farm buildings and slave quarters were in the *villa rustica*, at the back of the main villa.

PAINTING A FRESCO

The walls of the villa are decorated with paintings, called frescoes.

The artist first covers the wall with a smooth layer of new plaster.

He paints the background while the plaster is still quite damp.

When this is dry, he adds the foreground and the finishing touches.

His paints are made from plant and animal dyes, thickened with egg white.

Landscape scenes, portraits and myths are all popular fresco subjects.

Q

Does your house have its own toilet? If not where do you go when you need to use one?

Go to pages 24 & 29

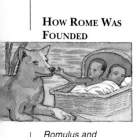

Romulus and Remus are left to die by the river Tiber. A she-wolf finds and rears them.

When they grow up, they decide to build a city at the place where the wolf found them.

They quarrel and Remus is killed. Romulus calls the city Rome and proclaims himself its first king.

Rome was founded in 753 BC. This famous statue shows the she-wolf suckling Romulus and Remus.

CITY OR COUNTRY?
WHAT WOULD YOUR LIFE BE LIKE?

(Above) *Dominating the city and river Tiber, was the Capitol, Rome's main temple. Below it, the Pons Sublicius crossed the Tiber in the heart of the city.*

(Above) *Roman towns and cities were laid out in a grid pattern, with their streets crossing at right angles.*

A ROMAN CITY was just like any other city – full of noise and hustle and bustle as people went to work, did the shopping or visited the baths. There were plenty of hazards awaiting you as you walked through the narrow city streets. You might have your pocket picked or be hit by an armful of rubbish thrown from the top floor of a nearby block of flats. In Rome, the streets got so crowded that no wheeled traffic was allowed during the day. At night, however, the clatter of cart wheels might well keep you awake.

Many of the city's public buildings – the *basilica*, temples and arches – were paid for by wealthy citizens, and often by the Emperor himself. If you had money, this was a good way of showing it off. But even if you didn't you were still proud of your great city.

Q

You are being posted abroad to the province of Dacia. Do you know where you are going to?

Go to page 19

BUILDINGS IN ROME

At the centre of every town is the forum – a large, open space used as a market and meeting place.

Each town or city has many different temples to the gods. The most important temple is usually in the forum.

No town, large or small, is complete without its baths (thermae). Some bathhouses are extremely grand.

Most cities have a theatre for plays and an amphitheatre for the ever popular gladiator fights and wild beast shows.

The basilica, or town hall, is the largest building in the forum. It contains offices and the local law courts.

Aqueducts carry water from distant springs into the town. A good water supply is essential for any city.

Rome was the biggest and most important city in the Empire. It had about one million inhabitants – a huge number for a city at this time.

PUBLIC BUILDINGS

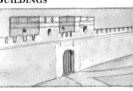

Walls show the sacred boundary of the city or town, marked out with a plough when it was founded.

Great victories are celebrated by the building of splendid triumphal arches. There are many such arches in Rome.

Roman towns have good drainage systems, with underground pipes and sewers carrying waste away.

The Romans were skilled civil engineers. Many of the bridges and aqueducts they built are still standing.

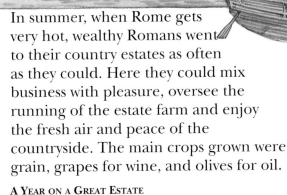

In summer, when Rome gets very hot, wealthy Romans went to their country estates as often as they could. Here they could mix business with pleasure, oversee the running of the estate farm and enjoy the fresh air and peace of the countryside. The main crops grown were grain, grapes for wine, and olives for oil.

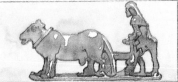

(Left) The ground is ploughed in late summer, ready for the wheat and barley to be sown.

A YEAR ON A GREAT ESTATE

The plough is pulled by a team of oxen, guided by a ploughman.

The plough is the only farm machine. Everything else is done by hand.

In late summer, the corn is harvested by slaves, using sharp sickles.

The harvest is loaded into an ox cart and taken to the granary.

The grain is sorted and ground into bread flour in the mill.

Then the estate's baker makes the first batch of hot, fresh bread.

MAKING WINE

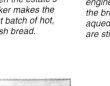

In the autumn, when the grapes were ripe, the slaves of the estate gathered them into wicker baskets.

The grapes were taken for pressing. This was done in a special wine press called a torculum.

As the pressure on the grapes increased, the juice was squeezed out and ran into a vat.

Top-quality wine was made from grapes dried in the sun for six days after they were picked.

When the wine was ready, it was put in barrels or earthenware jars. Each was labelled with the date.

Finally each barrel or jar was sealed, either with pitch or plaster. Wine was an important export.

Q

You have very hairy arms. How do you have the hair removed?

Go to page 23

You get up and join your family for prayers. Then you retire to the women's quarters.

Your job is to run the home. You tell the slaves what to cook for the feast later on.

YOUR FAMILY
WHAT WOULD YOURS BE LIKE?

YOUR PLACE in Roman society was strictly governed by who your parents were. People were divided into citizens and non-citizens. To qualify as a citizen, your parents had to be Romans born and bred. People were also granted citizenship, and the privileges that went with it, as a reward. If you were a non-citizen, your parents had probably been slaves or had been born in the provinces (the areas of the Empire outside Rome). Roman citizens were further divided into three classes – *nobiles* (aristocrats), *equites* (knights) and *plebeians* (commoners).

Roman citizens are encouraged to have large families. But it is not always possible. Many children die when they are still very young. And many mothers die in childbirth – there are no modern maternity hospitals.

In the afternoon, you send for your maid to help you style your hair and put on your make-up.

The family on the right are nobles. *Senators, consuls and magistrates normally come from rich, aristocratic families like this one.*

Sons often follow in their fathers' footsteps, whether to careers in politics or to hard-working lives as slaves.

Wherever a magistrate goes, he is escorted by lictors, men who carry the rods and axe symbolic of power.

You dress for dinner in new silk robes and your best jewellery. You are now ready to greet your guests.

Q

How old are you when your parents give you your name? What else are you given at the same time?

Go to page 40

A DAY AS A BUSY BUSINESSMAN

You get up early and put on your toga and sandals.

For breakfast, you have bread, cheese, honey and water.

You pray with your family at the household shrine.

You prepare a speech and dictate a couple of letters.

Your clients come to greet you and to ask your advice.

Then it's off to the forum for a chat with some friends.

Family life was very important. Your father was the head of the family, the *paterfamilias*. Your mother, brothers and sisters and any household slaves were all in his charge. If you had older brothers, their wives also became part of your family. Your father might have acted as a patron and given money and legal protection to people whose families were not influential. They were known as clients. In return, your father could count on their votes in elections for the Senate.

A POOR MAN'S WORKING DAY

You start your day very early. It's only just getting light when you get up to go to work.

Your breakfast consists of a plate of bread and olives. You cannot afford to have honey too.

The family above are equites, another group of upper-class Roman citizens. They have probably made their money in business or finance.

Equites *were originally cavalry officers in the Roman army. This is how they got their name. The Latin word* equus *means horse.*

(Below) Hedone, whose name is on this plaque, was the goddess of slaves.

Throughout the Roman Empire there are millions of slaves. If your parents are slaves, you, too, will be a slave. However, if your master is kind and you work well you may be able to buy or earn your freedom.

You might work on a food stall selling sizzling hot snacks for people to take away to eat.

The streets of Rome are thronged with people. Even if you don't know who they are, their clothes show the rank of society they belong to. In the same way your clothes will tell them the sort of family you come from. Among the crowds you will also see people from different provinces of the Empire. Their clothes look very odd among the togas and tunics of your fellow Romans.

PEOPLE OF THE ROMAN EMPIRE

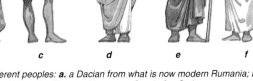

a   b   c   d   e   f   g   h

The Roman Empire is made up of many different peoples: **a.** a Dacian from what is now modern Rumania; **b.** Celtic-speakers from Gaul (France) or Britain; **c.** a Numidian from North Africa; **d.** a Roman citizen; **e.** a Greek; **f.** a Syrian woman; **g.** a Jewish priest from Judaea; **h.** a Palmyrene woman from Jordan.

At night, you go to bed as soon as it gets dark. You have too little money to waste on lamps.

Back home, you have a light lunch of bread and leftovers.

A short siesta, then a trip to the barber's for a hair cut.

In the afternoon there's more work to attend to.

After that is done, you set off for the baths to relax.

Later some friends and fellow business-men come to dinner.

It has been a busy day and you are ready for bed!

Q

You are on your way to the Circus Maximus. What are you going to see?

Go to page 31

First, pluck the flamingo. Then wash it, truss it (tie it up) and put it in a pan of lightly salted water.

Season with dill and a little vinegar. Bring to the boil, then simmer until the meat is tender.

Thicken the cooking liquid with flour to make a sauce. Flavour with mixed spices.

Finally, add the dates to the sauce. You can use the same recipe for cooking parrot.

Q

You have eaten far too much and now have stomach ache. What does the doctor give you for it?

Go to page 25

(Above) A Roman mosaic showing fish and shellfish.

FOOD AND DRINK
WHAT WOULD YOU EAT AND DRINK?

I F YOU THINK of Italian food today, you might think of pasta, tomatoes and red peppers as essential ingredients in Italian cooking. But as an ancient Roman, you would not have heard of these things. Bread, olives, olive oil and cheese would be the staple foods in your diet. Poor people received free bread from the state, which meant that vast quantities of grain had to be imported, largely from Egypt. There was no tea or coffee; you drank wine or water instead. Wine was always watered down. It was considered bad manners to drink it undiluted. The amount of meat or fish you ate depended on what you could afford. Pork and mutton were popular meats, though more exotic dishes, such as flamingo, were served at banquets.

(Above) A pestle and mortar for crushing spices.

(Below) Cooks could be hired from the public square if they were needed before a big banquet.

(Left) Some cooking utensils: **a.** wooden spoon, **b.** bronze grater, **c.** knife, **d.** bronze saucepan, **e.** bronze strainer and **f.** a metal utensil like an egg poacher.

(Above) Charcoal or wood was used for cooking.

(Below) Dinner party guests ate and drank from cups and shallow bowls like these. They were often made of silver.

Roman dinner parties are lavish affairs and an important part of a wealthy person's social life. The guests recline on three couches set around the table.

A RICH FAMILY'S DINNER PARTY

The triclinium (dining room) is decorated with fresh flowers for the party.

Your guests arrive. They bring their own table napkins with them.

Slaves wash the guests' hands. They also fan them as they eat.

The gustus (first course) is sows' udders stuffed with sea urchins.

A slave called a structor sets out the dishes for the next course.

Other slaves serve the wine. Only young slaves are allowed to do this.

Bread found in Pompeii.

As a member of a wealthy family, you had a kitchen in your house and slaves to do all the cooking for you. But if your family was poor you ate simple food, like bread and cheese, or bought hot food in the evening from a stall in the street. You drank water from the public fountains. Rich or poor, you usually ate your food with your fingers or a spoon.

A baker's shop with grain store (back), two mills (right) and oven.

A POOR FAMILY'S MEALS

You mainly eat bread, olives and grapes. You eat very little meat because it is so expensive.

You have your breakfast very early in the day. If you are very poor you may get free bread.

Lunch is at midday. You might eat vegetables left over from yesterday's dinner and also some fruit.

You have dinner before it gets dark. Your wife has bought it from the fast-food stall in the next street.

MAKING FISH SAUCE

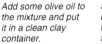

To make liquamen (fish sauce), mix some sprats with fish intestines.

Add some olive oil to the mixture and put it in a clean clay container.

Sprinkle with herbs. Leave it in the sun for three days to ferment.

Now strain the fish sauce and it is ready for you or your cook to use.

Women or slaves collect water from the public water fountains. It is a good opportunity to catch up with the latest gossip.

(Above) Fruit and vegetable sellers set up their stalls in the forum and streets on market days.

(Below) A customer picks a fresh goose from the butcher's shop. Sausages are also very popular.

Pottery jars (amphorae) sunk into the marble counter contain food or wine.

Poor people have no facilities for cooking. They buy meals from a fast-food shop or stall (thermopolium).

For the cena (main course), there may be ostrich, dormouse or flamingo.

The scissor cuts the guests' meat into convenient bite-sized pieces.

Guests may be sick between courses to make room for more food and drink!

The secunda mensa (desert) is served – fricassee of roses in flaky pastry.

The guests leave after midnight, with their napkins full of leftovers.

The slaves now have the task of clearing up all the awful mess.

Q

What would you eat if you were a legionary in the army? How much would your food cost you?

Go to page 36

YOUR CLOTHES

WHAT WOULD YOU WEAR?

(Above) Bracelet from Tunis, North Africa.

SKIN CARE

To soften your skin, you apply a cream made from wheat flour and asses' milk, or crushed snails.

It is fashionable to have pale skin. Skin whitener is made from a lead paste or from powdered chalk.

Roman women use crushed ants' eggs to highlight their eyebrows, or ash applied with the point of a needle.

Q

When would you start wearing a *toga virilis*? What special time does this mark in your life?

Go to page 26

THE MOST IMPORTANT article of clothing was the toga. However, you could only wear a toga if you were a citizen. Even then, the type of toga you wore depended on finer details, such as your age and status. On reaching the age of 14, boys were allowed to wear the pure white *toga virilis*. Younger boys and senators wore togas with a purple stripe. Many people found the toga heavy and cumbersome and preferred to wear simpler tunics for working and sleeping. Women wore under-tunics with long robes, called *stolas*, over the top.

(Above) Earrings may be made of gold, pearls or precious stones.

(Above) Necklaces, rings, bracelets and earrings are widely worn.

A poor man wears a loincloth and a simple tunic.

He fastens his belt and laces up his sandals.

If it is cold, a coarse wool cloak keeps him warm.

If you have a rich husband or father, your morning is spent having your hair styled and your make-up applied by your maids.

(Below) Essential toilet articles: **a**. perfume jars; **b**. bronze mirror; **c**. curling tongs; **d**. tweezers; **e**. make-up applicators and **f**. comb.

If you lived in a poor family your mother had little time or money to spend on her appearance. But if yours was a wealthy family she had time, money and slaves to help her look her best. No respectable woman went out without her hair, make-up and jewellery perfectly in place.

HAIR STYLES AND HAIR DRESSERS

Some wealthy women wear whole, false hairdos which are called galeri.

Slaves called cinerarii curl their mistress's hair with heated tongs.

Cinflones are slaves who dye hair by blowing powder on to it.

Some wealthy women dye their hair blonde or red, rather than leave it brown.

Psecas are slaves who scent hair by washing it with perfumed oils.

A woman tells the public torturer to beat a slave who has done her hair badly!

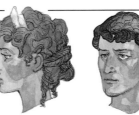

By the 3rd century BC, women's hairstyles are very elaborate.

It is often easier to wear a wig or a hairpiece fixed on with hairpins.

It is the fashion for men to be clean-shaven. Most have short hair.

WHAT DO YOU WEAR ON YOUR FEET?

In public, people wear leather boots held on by thongs. You can tell a senator by the crescent on the toe of his boot.

CLOTHES were usually made of wool or linen. Fine cottons and silk were expensive and so were only worn by the rich. Woollen togas were hot and uncomfortable in the summer and many people ignored the Emperor Augustus's decree that togas must be worn in public.

In private, people wear simpler sandals, tied with thongs and straps. They are much more comfortable.

(Left) A wealthy Roman couple in their best clothes. Roman clothes did not change much, except in small details.

PUTTING ON YOUR TOGA

Drape one end over your left shoulder so it reaches your ankles.

Most sandals are made of leather though poorer people also wear wooden sandals and sometimes clogs.

Put the other end under your right arm and over your left shoulder. Adjust so it's comfortable and pin firmly in place!

These shoes were found in Egypt. They cover the whole foot and are held on with leather laces.

HAIR CARE

To stop hair going grey, you apply oil mixed with earthworm ashes.

Dye hair black with lentils, wine and cypress leaves boiled with leeks.

Use bear fat or the ashes from hippopotamus skin to make hair grow.

Roman men go to special shops to get rid of hair from their arms.

Popular hair removers include bats' blood and hedgehog ashes.

Hair is also plucked out with tweezers or simply shaved off with a razor.

Q

What would you be doing and where would you be going wearing a dirty old toga on purpose?

Go to page 33

HAVING YOUR TOGA CLEANED

You don't have a washing machine. If you're rich, you send clothes to the fuller's to be cleaned.

First, the fuller hangs the clothes over round wooden frames and bleaches them with burning sulphur.

He puts them in a large vat of water and fuller's earth (a type of clay). He treads on them to get them clean.

Then he dries the clothes, folds and presses them to remove any creases. A slave collects them.

SICKNESS AND HEALTH

HOW WOULD YOU KEEP CLEAN AND HEALTHY?

HAVING A bath in ancient Rome was not simply a way of getting clean. It was an afternoon out – a chance to relax and socialize with friends. Most towns and cities had a public bathhouse. In big cities, these were very grand affairs, large enough to accommodate thousands of people. You didn't simply get in and out of a tub of water. You went through a series of hot and cold rooms, followed by a massage or a beauty treatment. If you were well-off, you took your own slave along to carry your towels and bathing things. It was also possible to hire an attendant for a small fee. The poor looked after themselves.

(Below) *The grandest of all bathhouses – the Baths of Caracalla in Rome. They were built by the Emperor Caracalla (ruled AD 211-217).*

Calidarium

Gymnasium

Tepidarium

Shops and offices

Frigidarium

Very few homes have toilets which flush, so you may have to use the public ones. You use a wet sponge on a stick instead of toilet paper.

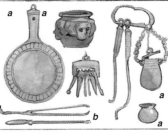

*Essentials for the baths: **a.** jars of the olive oil you put on your body and **b.** strigils to scrape off oil and dirt.*

HAVING A BATH

You leave your clothes in the apodyterium (the changing room).

Then it's time for a spot of training or exercise in the exercise yard.

The tepidarium is next – a warm room with a small bathing pool.

It's hotter and sweatier in the caldarium! You're glad of the pool.

Chatting to a friend takes your mind off the heat, but it's too hot to stay in long!

Ready for a shock? You plunge into the cold pool in the frigidarium!

Q

Why are snails so important for fashion conscious ladies?

Go to page 22

When people visit the temple of Aesculapius, they usually leave offerings shaped like the part of their body which is afflicted, like this ear and leg. These are tokens of thanks or reminders that help is still needed.

Library

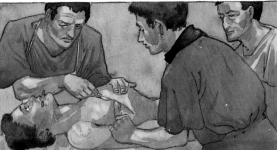

(Below) A surgeon's kit: **a.** medicine containers, **b.** speculum for internal examination, **c.** hooks for holding wounds open, **d.** probes, **e.** knives, **f.** spatulas and **g.** medicine spoons.

(Above) An operation in a military hospital.

Shops and offices

Gymnasium

A doctor examining a child.

Medicinal herbs:
a. Rosemary
b. Elecampane
c. Sage **d.** Garlic
e. Mustard seed

If you became ill, various treatments were available. There were skilled doctors, many of whom were Greek or had trained in military hospitals (like the one above). They usually treated illnesses such as stomach ulcers and asthma, with herbal medicines. They also carried out operations, giving the patient wine as an anaesthetic. But going to the doctor cost money. Instead, you might have tried the local chemist or spent a night in the temple of Aesculapius, god of healing. You hoped the god would visit you in your dreams and tell you how to get better.

You visit the doctor with stomach trouble. It must be something that you ate or drank.

The doctor examines you and asks questions about your diet and your way of life.

He prescribes a mustard gargle. Many Roman medicines are made from plants and herbs (see left).

You take your medicine home and take the first dose. It tastes awful so it must be good for you!

Q

You are a professional undertaker. What are your duties when a person has just died?

Go to page 41

After your bath, you are ready for a relaxing massage and a rest.

You buy a snack to eat from the restaurant, then you get dressed.

Some of the larger baths even have libraries and reading rooms.

There are also gardens and halls where you can stroll and chat.

There may even be a poetry recital or music concert for you to enjoy.

You've spent a happy afternoon at the baths, now it's time to go home.

Ink is made from fine soot and water, although tar and cuttlefish ink may also be used. Pens are made from reeds *(a)* or bronze *(b)*. A bronze stylus *(c)* is best for writing on wax tablets.

EDUCATION

WHAT WOULD YOU LEARN?

YOU WILL ONLY receive a good education if you are a boy and come from a wealthy family. If you have sisters their lessons will soon stop so your mother can teach them household duties in preparation for marriage. If your parents are poor, they cannot afford to send you to school. They need you to go out to work. Like most Romans you will be illiterate – unable to read or write.

If you do go to school, lessons last from dawn to midday. You will learn to read and write Latin and Greek, and to count using Roman numerals. Later, you will study the works of Greek and Roman playwrights, poets and philosophers.

EDUCATION FOR BOYS

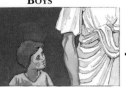

Only the sons of the wealthy have a good education. Boys of poor families learn how to make a living.

Both boys and girls are brought up from an early age to take part in religious ceremonies.

You start at the ludus (primary school) when you are 6. A slave takes you there.

At the age of 11, you move to the grammaticus. Here you study Greek, literature and public speaking.

(Above) Educated Romans could write Greek as well as Latin. This is part of a thank-you letter written in Greek.

(Above) Calculations are difficult to do in Roman numerals.

You are allowed to use an abacus to help you count.

These boys are from a very rich family. They are being taught at home by a Greek tutor known as a pedagogus. Although he is likely to be a slave, he is probably well educated.

You practise writing on a wax-covered board, using a pen called a stylus (top picture). It has a pointed end for writing and a blunt end for erasing errors.

THE TOGA VIRILIS

When a Roman boy is 14, he officially becomes an adult at a special ceremony held each year in March.

On this day, his parents give him his pure white toga virilis to put on for the first time. Now he is an adult.

He takes off his gold or leather bulla (childhood charm) before hanging it around the neck of his family god.

Then the whole family leads him to the Capitol or to another temple to offer sacrifices to the gods.

It is the feast of the god Bacchus. Priests and priestesses in ivy crowns sell sacred honey cakes to passers by.

The boy buys some cakes and places them on the altar as offerings to Bacchus, god of wine and honey.

Q

If you come from a rich family, where could you go to further your study of rhetoric?

Go to page 35

Girls usually stay at
home with their
mother. She teaches
them how to look
after and run the
house.

If you intend following a career in politics or the law, it is essential to learn rhetoric – the art of public speaking. For this, you will have to go to a special teacher, called a *rhetor*. He will teach you how to write speeches and the most persuasive ways of presenting them.

Reading a Roman book means rolling and unrolling a long scroll rather than turning over pages. Printing has not been invented, so books have to be copied out by hand, usually by Greek slaves. It is a slow and painstaking business and books are very expensive. There were plenty of bookshops in big cities, like Rome, as well as public libraries.

You will have a short break during lessons

Latin inscriptions are carved in stone using capital letters.

Public libraries are funded by the state or by rich individuals. They are the favourite meeting places of writers and literary critics.

They learn how to cook and how to spin and weave woollen cloth which is used to make clothes.

They may help their mother to look after their younger brothers and sisters. Slaves will do this if the family is rich.

(Above) *There are no books as we know them. Instead, authors write on long scrolls made from papyrus (an Egyptian reed) or parchment made from kid skin. The scrolls are kept in drum-like containers.*

At an early age, most girls are betrothed to be married. Many will die in childbirth before they are 30.

BECOMING A VESTAL VIRGIN

If you are a girl aged between 6-10 and from a good family, you may be chosen to become a Vestal Virgin.

You say goodbye to your friends. Your hair is cut and hung on a sacred tree outside the Temple of Vesta.

You cross the threshold of the temple and make your vows to stay for 30 years and not to marry.

For the first 10 years you are a novice. Then you spend the next 10 years guarding the sacred flame.

You spend the final 10 years training new Vestal Virgins. Then you are given your freedom and leave the temple.

It's not an easy life – you can only go out in a litter. But it is considered to be a great honour to be a Vestal Virgin.

Q

Which is the patron goddess of wisdom and crafts? What else is she the goddess of?
Go to page 39

Perhaps you are good at arguing your case and public speaking. A successful lawyer is highly respected.

You may be elected as a magistrate. Your job includes keeping law and order and collecting taxes.

You may be lucky enough to inherit a large estate from your father and so become a wealthy landowner.

Q

What is the *villa rustica*? Is it in the town or countryside? Who lives there and what do they do?

Go to page 15

CAREERS

WHAT WORK WOULD YOU DO?

THE CAREER you will follow depends entirely on the position of your family in Roman society. The only suitable careers for an upper-class Roman were in politics, the law or the army. If yours was a poorer family they were probably craftsmen or shopkeepers, and you would be, too.

Slaves, of course, had the hardest life of all. It wasn't too bad if you were a Greek slave – you might be employed as a private tutor or doctor. But for other slaves, life could be extremely harsh.

Career opportunities for women were rare. A very few became doctors and teachers; even fewer became Vestal Virgins and priestesses. Most women had no choice but to stay at home and keep house.

(Above) A knife cutter and his wife display their selection of wares – saws, knives and shears.

(Below) Animal bones and horns are made into everyday things, such as combs, needles and games' counters.

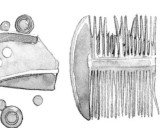

(Right) You can buy sandals off the shelf or have them made to measure.

(Above) The blacksmith makes ploughs, locks and tools to order.

People always need new sandals and the sandal-maker is kept busy.

(Below) There are smiths for working copper, bronze, iron, silver and gold. These are coppersmiths.

THE LOST WAX PROCESS

To make a bronze statue, an artist uses the 'lost wax' process. He makes a clay model of the statue.

He covers the clay model in wax and carves details on to the wax. He then adds another layer of clay.

The model is turned upside down and tubes attached for pouring in the liquid metal. Everything is covered in more clay.

The model is fired in an oven. The wax melts and runs off. Liquid metal is poured in to fill the gap.

The whole thing is left to cool, then the outer layer of clay (the mould) is broken. Inside is the bronze statue.

The artist then puts the finishing touches to the statue, carefully polishing it until the bronze shines.

(Above) A cloth merchant shows customers a length of finely-woven cloth.

(Below) Red Samian ware is popular. This type of pottery is made in Gaul (France).

SEXTIMA

Potter's stamp

Potter at work

(Right) Clay lamp with fishing scene.

(Left) The discovery that glass can be blown into bubbles, rather than just beaten flat means glass bottles and flasks are now cheaper.

Most busy streets in Rome were lined with shops and workshops. The shops opened out on to the street, while the craftsmen worked in the area at the back. A great variety of craftsmen was needed to keep the city supplied with goods. There were smiths, potters, sculptors, glass blowers, carpenters, masons, bone carvers and many more. If your father was a craftsman, he would pass on his skills and knowledge to you so that you could follow in his footsteps.

(Below) Stonemasons shape and decorate stone building blocks.

(Above) Carpenters make furniture or work on wooden buildings.

THE LIFE OF A SLAVE

You may be born a slave. Your grandparents were prisoners of war, sold by auction at the slave market.

You work on a large estate. Your kind owner treats you almost like one of the family. Not all slaves are so lucky.

Your master repays your loyalty and hard work. He gives you your own small patch of land to farm.

You are lucky! You will be looked after for life. Before the time of Augustus people got rid of their old slaves.

Q

You are a senator and have just ordered a new pair of sandals. What is special about them?

Go to page 23

THE FULLER'S WORK

A fuller's job is to clean clothes and to prepare lengths of cloth for making into new clothes.

He examines the cloth, then soaks it in urine (collected in pots in the street) to stiffen it.

Then the stiffened cloth is washed with fuller's earth to remove any dirt and grease from it.

The cloth is beaten and stretched to give it an even surface, then it is washed again in vats.

It is then rinsed, dried and taken to the roof. It is stretched over frames to bleach.

Finally, the fuller takes the cloth down to his front room where he presses it in a huge press.

You are on your way to the chariot races and buy a snack to keep you going. You support the Blue team.

You take your seat. The races are good for meeting girls as men and women sit together! The race begins.

The laps are marked by dolphins. The chariots, mostly driven by slaves, go past at speed.

In a thrilling finish, the Red team is the winner. Sometimes fans of the losing teams start riots.

Q

Under what circumstances would you have a triumphal arch raised in your honour?

Go to page 17

ENTERTAINMENT

HOW WOULD YOU HAVE FUN?

EVEN THOUGH you might have to work hard, there were plenty of public holidays when you could enjoy yourself. Romans were very fond of *ludi* (games), which were public entertainments put on and paid for by the government or wealthy nobles. There were three types of *ludi* – chariot races, theatrical performances, and gladiator fights and wild beast shows. This was entertainment on a very grand scale!

Professional musicians (slaves or freedmen) played at dinner parties and at the ludi. Instruments included lyres, flutes, cymbals, auloi (pipes), brass horns and rattles.

Charioteers are usually slaves. If they are successful, they become superstars. But they face great danger and even death.

Chariot racing was particularly popular. Thousands of people packed into the circus to cheer on their teams – the Blues, the Reds, the Greens or the Whites. Huge amounts of money were bet on these races.

Knucklebones is a popular game to play at home.

Games counter

The knucklebone pieces are goat or sheep bones.

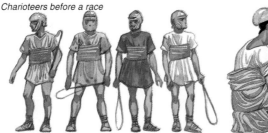

Charioteers before a race

GLADIATOR GAMES

A few days before the games, copies of the programme are put up around town by slaves of the senator paying for the games.

In the amphitheatre, there are special seats for the general public, women, senators and the Emperor himself.

The first fight is between a retiarius (left) and a murmillo (right). Gladiators are often slaves or prisoners.

The loser is at the public's mercy. A 'thumbs up' sign means the loser can live. 'Thumbs down' means death.

A gladiator of great courage is given a rudis (wooden stick). He hands in his weapons at the Temple of Hercules.

The next two gladiators on the programme arrive. They are both armed with helmets, shields and swords.

PUTTING ON A PLAY

The aedile (a junior official) hires the actors for one of the latest plays. He holds rehearsals in his own home.

On the day of the performance, a huge curtain is hung behind the stage. It is used to hide any scene changes.

One actor reads the prologue, a summary of the play. All the parts, male and female, are played by men.

The actors wear masks to show their characters. They also wear larger-than-life clothes and raised shoes.

The best seats are reserved for the senators. Women sit further back in case they fall in love with the actors!

The most popular plays are comedies, by playwrights such as Terence and Plautus. Tragedies are also performed.

At the end of the play, an actor asks for applause. But the audience quite often hiss and boo instead of clapping!

The actors wear masks to show the sort of character they are playing young, old, comic, tragic, male or female.

The Romans borrowed the idea of the theatre from the Greeks and, at first, the plays performed were Latin versions of Greek plays. Later, comedies by Roman playwrights became very popular.

Gladiator fights, however gory, were hugely popular. They were fights to the death, displays of strength and courage – qualities greatly admired by the Romans.

Crest

Bronze helmet

Flap protects neck

Flaps protect throat

Arm protectors

Sword

Shield

Greave protects leg

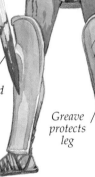

(Left) A murmillo waits for the fight to start.

(Below) A lamp showing the final moments of a fight. The victor prepares to kill his wounded opponent.

(Above) Wild animals are brought from all over the Empire to fight against gladiators or prisoners.

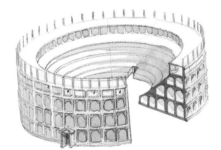

In Rome, gladiator fights are held in the Colosseum (left). This huge amphitheatre holds 50,000 spectators. The Circus Maximus in Rome is the main venue for chariot races.

(Right) Gladiator fights were seldom between evenly matched opponents. The murmillo (left) looks well armed, but his sword could get tangled in the net of the retiarius (centre), who could easily be killed by the spear of the velites (right).

When this fight is over, the herald announces a short interval. Time for you to get something to eat!

Some gladiators fight in groups. The opposing bands of velites stand apart and hurl missiles at each other.

When larger groups fight, the arena is turned into a battle field, strewn with dead, dying and wounded gladiators.

A gladiator armed only with a spear sizes up the lion he will have to fight. Which of them will win?

Two men dressed as Mercury and Pluto appear. Mercury sends the wounded to a doctor. Pluto kills the dying with a blow.

The dead bodies are thrown into a cave - the spolarium. Slaves drag them into the cave using large hooks.

Q

The festival of Saturnalia is looming up. What is in store for you if you are a slave?

Go to page 39

LAW AND ORDER

WOULD YOU OBEY THE LAW?

A CAREER IN POLITICS

If you are rich and ambitious, you may want to follow a career in politics. The army provides a good first step.

Your first government post is as a quaestor. This is a junior senator who deals with financial matters.

The next step on the ladder is the post of aedile. You look after the markets, public buildings and organize the games.

You may be elected a praetor and become a judge. Your job is to manage the law courts and decide who goes to trial.

Q

The fire brigade in Rome is kept busy day and night. Why is there such a risk of fire?

DURING THE REPUBLIC, the Senate had been Rome's governing body, made up of the heads of important upper-class families. They were voted into office each year by an Assembly of citizens. Later, ordinary citizens won the right to stand for office and have their say. After Augustus came to power, the Senate lost some of its influence. The Emperor became the all-powerful head of state. Augustus, the first Emperor of Rome, governed with the Senate's support. Others were not so wise. Caligula outraged senators when he insisted on having his horse elected consul – one of the highest political positions.

The basilica was the largest and most impressive building in the forum of any Roman town or city. It served as town hall and law court. The central hall, surrounded by a colonnade and passages was a popular meeting place for citizens.

In the provinces, travelling tax collectors make sure that people pay what they owe to the government. Taxes help pay for the upkeep of the army.

DURING THE REPUBLIC

As Rome becomes more and more powerful the legal system gets very complicated. A huge code of laws develops.

Under the Republic the laws are made by the Senate and by the Assemblies (groups of Roman citizens).

Some of these laws are rather vague! In court, a judge has to decide how best to apply them to the case before him.

Each new judge issues a document about how he interprets the laws. This is called an edictum.

Legal books contain written details, useful advice and learned commentaries on all the various trials and verdicts.

Laws vary in the different provinces because the governors take local laws and customs into account in their judgements.

Go to page 14

CRIMES AND PUNISHMENTS

Army discipline is very strict. Woe betide you if you break the rules. Deserters face the death penalty. If a whole unit deserts its post, one in every ten soldiers is executed. This type of punishment is called decimation. For lesser crimes, you might be demoted or given extra, unpleasant, duties such as cleaning the latrines.

(Left) You may have to pay a fine or compensation as punishment for not honouring debts or for fraud.

For more serious crimes, you may be exiled or even lose your citizenship, and that is a dreadful punishment.

Some criminals are sent to work down the mines or as oarsmen on ships. Many are badly treated and die.

(Above) A deserter is stoned or beaten to death by his comrades. This is because he has put their lives in danger by his cowardice.

(Below) The worst crimes, such as treason, receive the death penalty. Some criminals are beheaded; others are crucified on a wooden cross.

(Above) Famous emperors: **a.** Augustus (27 BC–AD 14), **b.** Tiberius (AD 14-37), **c.** Caligula (AD 37-41), **d.** Claudius (AD 41-54), **e.** Nero (AD 54-68), **f.** Domitian (AD 81-96), **g.** Trajan (AD 98-117), **h.** Hadrian (AD 117-138), **i.** Septimius Severus (AD 193-211), **j.** Caracalla (AD 211-217), **k.** Diocletian (AD 284-305), **l.** Julian the Apostate (AD 360-363).

A COURT CASE

Any private citizen can accuse someone of a crime and summon them to court. You can use force if necessary!

The jury is sworn in and the trial begins. If the crime is serious, you can pay a lawyer to speak for you.

The accused person sometimes puts ashes in his hair and wears rags or dirty clothes to get the jury's sympathy.

Everyone speaks, then the jury votes the accused guilty or not guilty. The judge announces the punishment.

Like any big city, plenty of crimes were committed in Rome. It was not particularly safe to walk the streets at night for fear of being robbed. Wealthy Romans had bars on their windows, or guard dogs, to deter would-be burglars. Some houses had the Roman equivalent of 'Beware of the Dog' signs – mosaics with the words CAVE CANEM.

JESUS CHRIST'S CRUCIFIXION was ordered by the Roman governor of Judaea, Pontius Pilate. Only criminals without Roman citizenship were crucified. Death was slow and painful.

Footrest

Upright beam

Long iron nails through wrist

Sign giving victim's name and crime

Crossbar weighing about 60 kilos. The prisoner had to carry it to the place of execution

Rome has its own fire brigade and police force, the cohortes vigilum. Fires are very frequent in Rome.

LAW REFORMS UNDER THE EMPIRE

When Augustus becomes Emperor there is a great change. Now the Emperor devises many of the laws.

Some laws are still made by the Senate. But the Emperor has to add his seal of approval for them to be passed.

Judges have less authority and power, although they still issue their personal interpretations of the various laws.

During Augustus' reign, judges have to listen to and obey the opinions of lawyers appointed by the Emperor.

Emperor Hadrian has all the regional variations of laws collected together, listed and made to follow a standard.

All Roman citizens, wherever they live in the Empire, have to obey the reformed laws drawn up by Hadrian.

Q Army discipline is strict, but the rewards for loyal service are good. What are they?

Go to page 37

TRAVEL AND TRADE

WHERE WOULD YOU GO?

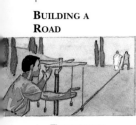

The surveyor choses the shortest, straightest route for the road. He measures this using a groma.

To make the road, a trench about a metre deep is dug. It is filled with rubble and surfaced with gravel or stones.

The road has a curved surface (camber) so that rainwater drains away and does not form puddles.

Each mile is marked by a mile stone. A Roman mile is a thousand paces, or about 1,460 metres in length.

Q

You have never seen a bar of soap. Instead you use olive oil to get yourself clean. How?

Go to page 24

AS THE ROMAN EMPIRE expanded, and more and more territory came under Roman rule, the world opened up to traders and travellers. The huge road system had already been started – it eventually covered over 85,000 kilometres. Roads were built so that the army could move quickly from place to place but civilians benefited too. If you had to go on a long journey, now was the time to do it. The army maintained the *Pax Romana* (Roman Peace) and kept the roads safer than they ever had been before, although highwaymen were still about. There were even guide books available, giving you lists of places to stay and road maps. Merchants took advantage of the improved communications, and trade with the provinces flourished.

Canvas or leather sail

Merchant ships dock at Ostia. There, they are unloaded and their cargoes carried by smaller boats up the river Tiber to Rome. The river is not wide or deep enough for the merchant ships to travel further up it.

Amphorae stored in hold below deck

TYPES OF TRANSPORT

     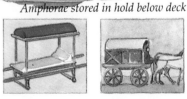

A packhorse or mule is the cheapest form of transport if you are only going a short distance.	*Out in the countryside, oxen or mules pull carts loaded with goods to and from the market.*	*A covered, horse-drawn wagon gives you more speed and shelter, but riding is faster.*	*If you are rich, you may be able to afford a carriage called a carpentum for trips into town.*	*Wealthy women are carried through the streets in sedan chairs, by slaves known as lecticarii.*	*Horses and carts carry the government post from town to town. The horses are often changed.*

Cargo was also carried by sea. The port of Ostia, near Rome, was always busy. Ships unloaded wheat from Egypt, olive oil from Spain, wool from Britain and exotic, wild animals from Africa. Sea crossings were carefully planned. No one sailed in winter – the weather was too bad. Even in summer, you risked being attacked by pirates.

The best olive oil is imported from Spain. A merchant ladles out oil for a customer (above).

As trade grows, coins replace bartering and the money system is standardized.

The first Roman warships were copies of ships from Carthage in North Africa. Now the Romans have a great fleet of ships called triremes. These warships have three tiers of oars, pulled by slaves.

Cabin

Smaller boats unload cargoes

Oar for steering

PERILS OF TRAVEL

Watch out! You might be kidnapped and sold as a slave in a foreign land far away from your home and family.

Shipwreck. False signals are sent out to confuse navigators so they sail their ships on to the rocks.

Always consult a soothsayer before you embark on a journey to see if the time is right to travel.

Never travel alone if you can help it and, if possible, always stay with friends, not at a strange inn.

WHERE COULD YOU TRAVEL TO?

You might travel to Hispania (Spain) to take advantage of the good weather and the excellent olive oil!

Gaul is made up of most of modern France. It has the advantage of being quite close and its wines are improving!

Germania, as its name suggests, covers Germany and parts of modern Holland, Belgium and the Alps.

Britain might seem a bit cold if you're used to the heat of Rome. It's worth visiting Hadrian's Wall in the north.

If you're after adventure, Egypt might be the place for you. Take a trip to visit the amazing pyramids.

You might be sent to Athens, Greece, to study Greek and rhetoric if your family are very well off. It will help your career.

Q

Mules are a common form of transport in ancient Rome. But what is so special about Marius's mules?

Go to page 37

The testudo

WHAT WOULD A SOLDIER'S LIFE BE LIKE?

THE MAIN REASON for Rome's success and expansion was its army – the biggest and best of its time. Soldiers were posted to every corner of the Empire to put down rebellions and guard the frontiers. During times of peace, they lived in stone or timber forts where they continued to train and drill and prepare for war. It was not as exciting as the real thing, and you might have found yourself longing for a skirmish if it was peaceful for too long.

If you were a Roman citizen, you could join the army as a legionary. Non-citizens joined up as auxiliaries. Each legion had about 5,000 soldiers, divided into smaller units of 80 men, called centuries. You marched into battle behind your legion's standard – a silver *aquila* (eagle).

Roman general

Roman centurion

JOINING UP

You've decided – you're joining the army. It is a big step to take. You have to sign on for 25 years.

You are a Roman citizen so you are made a legionary. You begin your army life in Rome, training to fight.

Training is hard work. But you survive and are posted to the Rhine for your first duty abroad.

Your first real battle. The Romans win and send loot and prisoners of war back to Rome to become slaves.

(Above) When you join up, you swear an oath of loyalty to the Emperor. Then you are given your uniform.

Tent of leather

Food is strictly rationed. Each bread issue is stamped **(above)**.

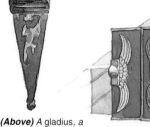

(Above) A gladius, a legionary's short, stabbing sword in its scabbard. This and his javelins are his main weapons.

YOU HAVE to spend about a third of your wages on food. Meals are simple – bread, cheese and pulses (peas, beans and lentils), washed down with cheap wine.

Q

You are a sentry in the army and you have deserted your post. What will happen to you if you're caught?

Go to page 33

EARLY YEARS

The army returns to Rome in triumph. You march proudly in the victory procession through the streets.

But there's no peace for new army recruits. You soon find yourself setting sail for Britannia (Britain).

You are sent to Hadrian's Wall, the northernmost border of the Empire in Britain. It's a long march.

Work begins on building a fort behind the wall. This is to be your headquarters and home for the winter.

Winter arrives, freezing cold. You ask the scribe to write to your family asking for some food and warm underwear.

Your main job in Britain is to assist with a great building programme. You help to build a new road.

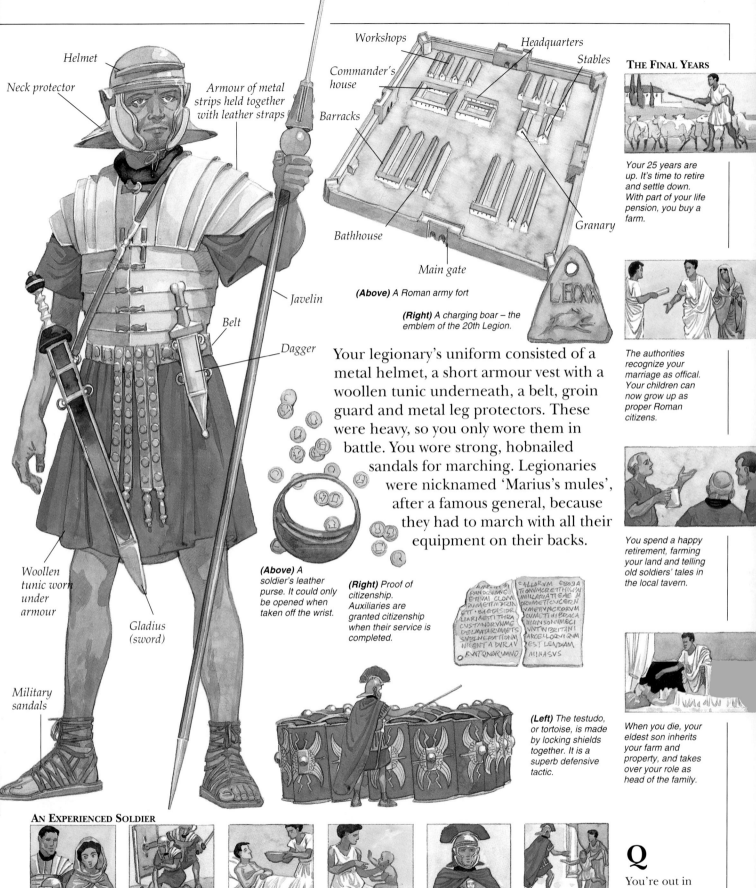

Helmet

Neck protector

Armour of metal strips held together with leather straps

Javelin

Belt

Dagger

Woollen tunic worn under armour

Gladius (sword)

Military sandals

Workshops

Headquarters

Commander's house

Stables

Barracks

Granary

Bathhouse

Main gate

(Above) A Roman army fort

(Right) A charging boar – the emblem of the 20th Legion.

LEGXX

Your legionary's uniform consisted of a metal helmet, a short armour vest with a woollen tunic underneath, a belt, groin guard and metal leg protectors. These were heavy, so you only wore them in battle. You wore strong, hobnailed sandals for marching. Legionaries were nicknamed 'Marius's mules', after a famous general, because they had to march with all their equipment on their backs.

(Above) A soldier's leather purse. It could only be opened when taken off the wrist.

(Right) Proof of citizenship. Auxiliaries are granted citizenship when their service is completed.

(Left) The testudo, or tortoise, is made by locking shields together. It is a superb defensive tactic.

THE FINAL YEARS

Your 25 years are up. It's time to retire and settle down. With part of your life pension, you buy a farm.

The authorities recognize your marriage as offical. Your children can now grow up as proper Roman citizens.

You spend a happy retirement, farming your land and telling old soldiers' tales in the local tavern.

When you die, your eldest son inherits your farm and property, and takes over your role as head of the family.

AN EXPERIENCED SOLDIER

Like many fellow soldiers, you marry a local girl, though the army disapproves. Your wife adopts Roman ways.

Then disaster strikes. You are badly wounded in a skirmish with a war-like local tribe and almost die.

You spend several weeks in the army hospital. This is housed in a large tent. You make a complete recovery.

Soon afterwards, your wife has a baby son. You live with your family in the settlement outside the fort.

An experienced soldier, you are now promoted to the rank of centurion in charge of a unit of 80 men.

Trouble flares up suddenly in the Rhine and you are sent abroad. You return safely, but years later.

Q

You're out in the provinces. An auxiliary asks you how Rome was founded. Can you remember?

Go to page 16

THE ARMY 37

WAYS OF
WORSHIP

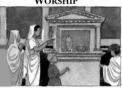

At home, you have a small shrine where your family prays every day to Vesta, goddess of the home and hearth.

The shrine contains figures of the lares and penates. These spirits watch over your household.

The harsupex is a priest who looks at the livers of sacrificed animals to discover the will of the gods.

Special chickens are kept. If they eat well, it is a good omen. If they eat very little, it means the gods are angry with you.

Q

How does a girl become a Vestal Virgin? What are your duties and what must you never do?

Go to page 27

THE GODS

WHAT WOULD YOU BELIEVE IN?

THE ANCIENT ROMANS believed in many different gods and goddesses. These were split into two groups. Roman homes were protected by household gods – the *lares*, who were the family's ancestral spirits, and the *penates*, who looked after the larder. They were worshipped every day at the household shrine, the *lararium*.

The gods in the second group were those of the official state religion. Many of these were based on Greek gods which the Romans had adopted. Different gods looked after different aspects of life. For example, you prayed to Mars, the god of war, for success in battle. People feared the gods and tried to keep them happy with offerings and sacrifices. If things went wrong, they believed it was because the gods were angry.

Jupiter is the king of the gods and god of the sky, thunder and lightning. His special symbols are an eagle or a thunderbolt.

Altar on which a fire will be lit

TEMPLES are seen as the homes of the gods, and house their statues. The temple priests conduct rituals and sacrifices to win the gods' favour. Animals are sacrificed on an altar in front of the temple.

Bull to be killed for the sacrifice

Priest carrying axe for the sacrifice

Procession of priests

SYMBOLS OF
GOOD AND EVIL

Like everyone else you are very superstitious. Owls may signal disaster.

Bald men may stop their hair falling out by sniffing cyclamen flowers!

The sound of bells is thought to ease the pain of women in childbirth.

Bees are sacred messengers of the gods and symbols of good luck.

Peony flowers have special, magical powers of healing the sick and ill.

Eagles, emblems of the Roman legions, are said to bring thunderstorms.

People in the provinces were allowed to carry on worshipping their own local gods as long as they also worshipped the Roman state gods. Some Romans found the state religion too stuffy and impersonal and turned instead to cults from the east which seemed more positive. Some of these cults promised their followers life after death.

There were religious festivals every month in honour of particular gods and goddesses. Many of these were public holidays and games were held in celebration.

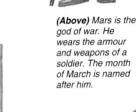

(Above) Mars is the god of war. He wears the armour and weapons of a soldier. The month of March is named after him.

(Above) Juno is Jupiter's wife and sister. She is the goddess of women and of childbirth. Her special symbol is a peacock.

(Right) Minerva is the goddess of wisdom, war and crafts. She is shown with a helmet and spear.

(Above) Diana, goddess of the moon and hunting.

(Above) Venus, the goddess of love and beauty.

(Above) Isis, originally an Egyptian goddess.

(Right) The cult of Mithras comes from Persia and is very popular with Roman soldiers. Here Mithras slays a bull whose blood is the lifeblood of the universe.

(Right) Bacchus is one of the most popular gods – the god of wine. His symbol is a bunch of grapes.

(Right) Pan is one of the Greek gods which the Romans have adopted. Half man, half goat, he is the god of the mountains. He always appears with his pipes.

FIGURES IN RELIGION

Temple priests perform the sacrifices and conduct religious ceremonies. There are priestesses too.

Temple priests perform the sacrifices and conduct religious ceremonies. There are priestesses too.

The Vestal Virgins look after the sacred fire in the temple of Vesta. It must never be allowed to go out.

In times of national crisis government officials consult the prophecies of a priestess called the Sibyl.

From the time of Augustus, the Emperor himself holds the position of Chief Priest (Pontifex Maximus).

Q

If you were a wounded gladiator, which god would you rather have on your side – Mercury or Pluto?

Go to page 31

SATURNALIA

The Saturnalia festival is held in December. It began as a celebration to mark the end of the planting season. It is now one of the merriest Roman festivals.

During the Saturnalia, slaves have their freedom for a few days.

They are waited on at dinner by their masters, just for a welcome change.

People give each other gifts, such as wax candles and small dolls.

A mock-king is crowned. His job is to preside over the festival.

BIRTH, MARRIAGE AND DEATH
WHAT HAPPENS WHEN YOU ARE BORN, GET MARRIED OR DIE?

A new-born baby is bathed by its nurse, then carried to its father and placed at his feet.

If the father takes the child into his arms, it shows he accepts responsibility for its upbringing.

(Above) The dextrarium iunctio (joining of hands) ceremony. The bride-to-be wears a ring on the third finger of her left hand. A nerve is thought to run directly to the heart from here.

A S AN ANCIENT ROMAN, your life was marked by special festivals and ceremonies to celebrate important events such as your birth, marriage or death. You celebrated your birthday each year with offerings to your household gods and a family feast. The Emperor's birthday was a national holiday.

Your marriage was arranged by your parents – you had little say in it. Many marriages were arranged for financial or political reasons. Girls married young, at 13 or 14. Boys were usually older. The girl's parents had to hand over a dowry of money, clothes and household goods to the groom's family. A woman only regained control of her property if her husband died. For this reason, women who had been widowed were often reluctant to remarry.

If a man divorces his wife for no reason, he has to hand back her dowry.

If he divorces her because she is unfaithful, he keeps the dowry.

If the baby is not accepted by its father, or is weak or deformed, it is abandoned and left to die.

(Below) At the wedding, the bride and groom exchange vows.

The baby is named at a ceremony nine days after its birth. It is also given a bulla (lucky charm).

MARRIAGE

Q
Your family have the social rank of *nobiles*. Why is this a good thing for you and your future?

Go to page 18

Your parents hope you will be happy, but do not think it very important.

The bride-to-be's ring was usually fairly plain, to symbolize her virtue.

The wedding day is chosen with care. The second half of June is a lucky time.

On the eve of the wedding, the bride offers her toys to the household gods.

The bride's wedding dress is a white toga, with a bright orange veil over her head.

The couple sit on stools while the marriage contract is read and sealed.

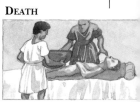

If a wealthy person dies, their ashes are placed in a marble or glass urn inside the family tomb. Poor people are cremated or buried communally. A coffin to transport the body has to be rented.

DEATH

When a person dies, professional undertakers come to prepare the body for burial or cremation.

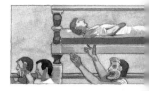

They wash and embalm the body and dress it in a toga, together with any symbols of public office.

On the day of the funeral, the body is placed on a litter and carried in a procession to its burial place.

MORE THAN DEATH
itself, Romans feared dying unmourned and unburied. Many people arranged and paid for their funerals well in advance. The best way to die was surrounded by your family. Your eldest son placed a coin in your mouth to pay the ferryman who would take you over the river Styx from the land of the living to Hades, the world of the dead.

(Left) funeral procession carved on a tombstone.

Funeral procession led by flute players. Only the rich had funerals. The body was carried to the grave in a litter along a path lined with tombstones. The dead person's family follow.

In a cremation, the body is burned on a funeral pyre. Burials can only take place outside the city boundary.

In the evening, there is a great feast at the bride's father's house.

The wedding cake, made of pastry soaked in sweet wine, is served.

Then, the bride, groom and guests proceed to the groom's house.

The bride daubs oil on the door and hangs ribbons on the door post.

The bride is lifted over the threshold of the house by her bridegroom.

She is given a lighted torch and some water as symbols of purity.

Q
You have lent some money and they are refusing to pay it back. How do you take them to court?

Go to page 33

HOW DO WE KNOW?

This bronze dog tag gives the owner's name and address (Viventius on the estate of Callistus) and asks the finder to return the dog.

I N THE 3RD CENTURY AD, chinks began to appear in the Roman Empire's armour. Power struggles and a weakening of the army's influence paved the way for barbarian tribes such as the Franks, Visigoths and Vandals to invade Roman territory. In AD 285, the Empire was split into west and east by Emperor Diocletian. Although the two parts were reunited in the fourth century, the western half steadily declined. Rome was sacked by the Visigoths in AD 410. However, the eastern half of the Empire thrived for hundreds of years more as the Byzantine Empire.

The Roman Empire stretched far and wide and left a huge amount of archaeological evidence – buildings, bones, coins and pottery. There is also a wealth of Latin literature which provides details of daily life, military strategy and successes, the legal system and so on. The revival of interest in things Classical (Roman and Greek) began with the 15th-century Renaissance in Europe and still continues.

(Left) Portrait medallion of Augustus, the first Roman Emperor.

(Left) Almost 2000 years ago a newly freed slave celebrated by setting up this plaque to Hedone, goddess of slaves. Today, what it tells us about the Roman Empire is as important as coins showing Roman Emperors *(below)*.

(Above) Tombs of rich people are often decorated with marble portraits of the deceased and inscriptions of their names and dates.

(Right) Roman coins have been found as far afield as India.

(Below) Latin inscription from the Temple of Augustus in Ankara, Turkey. It is Augustus's account of his reign and an important historical source. Inscriptions like this have been found all over the area occupied by the Romans. They help to add to our knowledge of the Romans and their Empire.

(Left) Copy of a document granting Roman citizenship to someone born in the provinces.

THE STORY OF POMPEII

In the 1st century AD, Pompeii was a prosperous town beside the Bay of Naples.

The Romans had captured this part of Italy from the Etruscans in 80 BC.

In AD 62, Pompeii was badly damaged when a strong earthquake struck the area.

Then, in AD 79, the volcano Vesuvius erupted burying Pompeii in lava and ash.

(Below) The Pantheon, Rome. The building of this huge temple to honour all the Romans' gods was begun around AD 120 on the orders of the Emperor Hadrian. Its huge dome is yet another demonstration of the Romans' building, engineering and architectural skills.

(Below) This Briton was killed by a ballista missile through his spine.

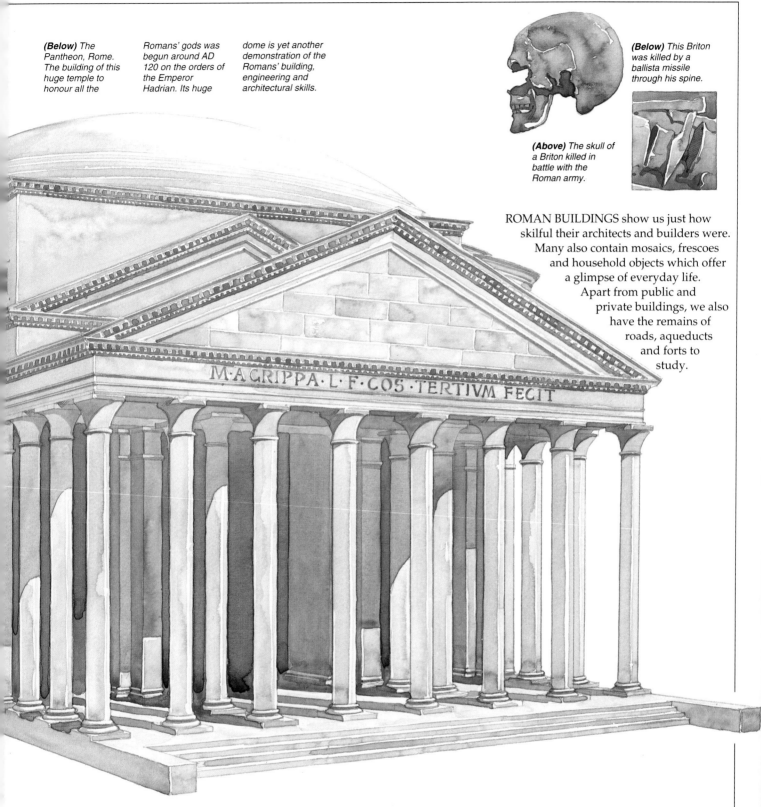

(Above) The skull of a Briton killed in battle with the Roman army.

ROMAN BUILDINGS show us just how skilful their architects and builders were. Many also contain mosaics, frescoes and household objects which offer a glimpse of everyday life. Apart from public and private buildings, we also have the remains of roads, aqueducts and forts to study.

Pompeii never recovered from the disaster and was almost forgotten.

In 1748, the King of Naples began to excavate the ruins of Pompeii.

Many mosaics, fine frescoes and sculptures have been uncovered.

The remains of villas, streets and the forum have also been found.

The archaeologist, Giuseppe Fiorelli, made plaster casts from actual objects.

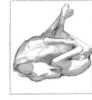

This is a plaster cast of a dog which was buried as it was chained up.

Today, visitors to Pompeii can walk back in time into an ancient Roman city.

TIMESPAN

THE HISTORY OF ANCIENT ROME IS divided into two main periods. The Roman Republic began in about 510 BC and continued until the death of Julius Caesar in 44 BC. Power struggles and civil war followed. In 27 BC, the first Roman Emperor, Augustus, seized power and the period known as the Roman Empire began.

The date traditionally given for the founding of Rome is 753 BC. The city grew from a group of villages founded on the seven hills beside the river Tiber by tribal people who had migrated into Italy from central Europe over a thousand years before. Legend has it that the first king of Rome was Romulus, one of the twin brothers found and raised by a she-wolf. Six other kings succeeded Romulus. In about 510 BC, the last of the kings, Tarquinius Superbus (Tarquin the Proud) was driven out of the city and Rome became a republic. (A republic is a country which is not ruled by a king or emperor but is governed by a group of officials elected by the people.)

510 BC – 27 BC The Roman Republic. Rome gradually emerges as the dominant power in the region. In 390 BC, Rome is invaded and plundered by the Gauls (from France). It slowly recovers. The city is rebuilt and reinforced, and the army is strengthened. By 285 BC, Rome has fought against and beaten the Gauls, Samnites and Etruscans (two peoples from southern Italy). By 264 BC, Rome controls the whole of Italy.

The Punic Wars (264-241 BC, 218-201 BC and 149-146 BC). The major threat to Rome's expansion in the Mediterranean are the Carthaginians from North Africa. The Romans and Carthaginians fight three wars, called the Punic Wars. In the last one, the Romans defeat Hannibal, the Carthaginian leader, and destroy the city of Carthage which becomes a Roman province. By 31 BC, most of the countries which border the Mediterranean have fallen to Rome's power.

58-44 BC Julius Caesar conquers Gaul and becomes Rome's greatest ruler yet. A group of senators, led by Brutus and Cassius, resent Caesar's power. On 15 March 44 BC, they murder him in the Senate.

44-27 BC Civil war between forces led by Mark Antony and Octavian, who Julius Caesar had appointed as his heir.

27 BC - AD 14 The Roman Empire is established. Julius Caesar's adopted son, Octavian, defeats his rival, Mark Antony and his lover, the Egyptian queen Cleopatra, and becomes the first Emperor of Rome. He takes the name Augustus, which means 'revered one'. From now until his death in AD 14, peace reigns in Rome and the Roman Empire overseas is expanded.

AD 14-53 The Roman Empire continues to grow, largely due to the work of Augustus in developing an efficient civil service and strong government in the provinces.

AD 54-68 The reign of Emperor Nero during which the Great Fire destroys two-thirds of Rome in AD 64. The Emperor is supposed to have played his lyre and watched as the city went up in flames.

AD 69-96 The reigns of Emperors Vespasian, Titus and Domitian are knows as the Flavian Dynasty. Vespasian orders the building of the Colosseum in Rome.

AD 98-117 Reign of Emperor Trajan. The Empire reaches its greatest extent with the conquest of Dacia (Rumania) and parts of the Middle East.

AD 117-138 Reign of Emperor Hadrian, Trajan's successor. Hadrian gives up some of the new provinces, believing the Empire is becoming too big and unwieldly. He concentrates on fortifying the borders. Hadrian's Wall is one of the fortifications.

AD 138-180 This work is continued by the next two Emperors, Antoninus Pius and Marcus Aurelius.

AD 193-211 Emperor Septimius Severus establishes firm control after a period of unrest and civil war.

AD 235-268 Time of great unrest within the Roman Empire and increasing attacks on its frontiers, especially in the north and east.

AD 284-305 Reign of Emperor Diocletian after another period of chaos, civil war and invasion. He splits the Empire into two – the Western Empire and the Eastern Empire.

AD 312-337 Emperor Constantine founds the city of Constantinople (modern Istanbul). It becomes the capital of the Eastern Empire which later becomes known as the Byzantine Empire. Christianity has spread throughout the Roman Empire by this time, but Christians risk persecution. In 313 Constantine announces that Christianity is to be tolerated. In 380 it becomes the official religion of the Empire under Theodosius I.

AD 406-476 The Western Empire is overrun by barbarian tribes and collapses. Rome is invaded and destroyed; the last Western Emperor, Romulus Augustulus, is deposed.

AD 527-565 Justinian, ruler of the Eastern Empire, regains much of Rome's lost territory but, within a century or so, Rome again loses control of most of it.

The Eastern Empire is weakened by the spread of Islam but survives until AD 1453 when Constantinople is conquered by the Muslim leader of Turkey, Sultan Mehmet II.

HAVE YOU SURVIVED?

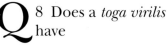

Q1 You're consulting a *haruspex*. Are you

A having your eyes tested?
B discovering the will of the gods?
C deciding what to have for dinner?

Q2 Is a *strigil*

A an instrument of torture?
B a popular song?
C something for scraping off dirt?

Q3 Someone asks you which you like best - the Blues, the Reds, the Greens or the Whites. Are they talking about

A political parties?
B chariot racing?
C the latest 'in' colours for clothes?

Q4 A *bulla* is

A a lucky charm?
B someone to avoid?
C a type of ox?

Q5 Who found and raised Romulus and Remus:

A the Emperor Augustus?
B Julius Caesar?
C a she-wolf?

Q6 Would you use fuller's earth to

A get your clothes clean?
B pot plants in?
C thicken soups and sauces?

Q7 If you decided to join the army, would you swear an oath of allegiance to

A Jupiter?
B your father?
C the Emperor?

Q8 Does a *toga virilis* have

A a red stripe?
B no stripe at all?
C a purple stripe?

Q9 Do aqueducts carry

A passengers?
B water?
C germs?

Q10 You want to soften your skin. Would you use

A asses' milk?
B olive oil?
C crushed ants' eggs?

Q11 What should you always do before a journey:

A have the hair on your arms removed?
B have a good night's sleep?
C consult a soothsayer?

Q12 You want to learn the art of public speaking. Do you go to

A a *rhetor*?
B a *lictor*?
C a *quaestor*?

Q13 If you were a *scissor*, would your job be

A styling people's hair?
B teaching Latin?
C cutting up food?

Q14 Does Samian ware come from

A Hispania?
B Gaul?
C Dacia?

TO FIND OUT what your survival rating is *go to page 48.*

GLOSSARY

AMPHITHEATRE an oval arena, surrounded by seats where gladiator and wild beast shows were held.

AMPHORA a pottery jar for storing and carrying wine, olive oil and fish sauce.

AQUEDUCT a large bridge with a channel running across the top which brought water supplies into the town from the countryside.

AQUILA the silver eagle standard which was carried before a legion when it went into battle or was on the march. If the eagle was captured, the legion fell.

ATRIUM the central courtyard of a Roman house, with an open roof (*compluvium*) and a pool beneath for collecting rainwater (*impluvium*).

BALLISTA a missile launcher which shot iron missiles at the enemy.

BASILICA a large building in the *forum*, used as a town hall and law court.

BULLA a lucky charm which Roman children wore around their necks to ward off evil spirits.

CAMEO a carving of a person's portrait or special symbol on a brooch or ring.

CENA the main meal of the day, eaten in the late afternoon. The word also referred to the main course.

CIRCUS the arena in which chariot races took place.

CITIZEN a Roman who had the right to vote to elect people to the Senate and to political posts in the Senate. He also had the right to wear a toga and serve as a legionary in the army.

CLIENT a freed man or a man without a family of his own who attached himself to an established family for legal and financial protection.

CONSUL the highest political post in the time of the Republic. Two consuls were elected each year. They managed the senate's affairs and commanded the army.

DOMUS a private town house, affordable only by very wealthy Romans.

ESTATE a *villa* and all the farmland belonging to it.

FORUM a town's central meeting and market place. The town's most important buildings and temples were usually in the *forum*.

FREED MAN a slave who had been released by his master or had bought his freedom.

FRESCO a wall painting in which the paint is applied while the plaster covering the wall is still wet.

FULLER a person who cleaned clothes and prepared cloth for making into clothes.

GROMA an instrument used by a surveyor or architect for measuring straight lines.

INSULA any area or block of a Roman town or city surrounded by streets. The word initially meant 'island'. The Americans use 'block' in a similar way today. (Plural: *insulae*.)

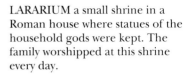

LARARIUM a small shrine in a Roman house where statues of the household gods were kept. The family worshipped at this shrine every day.

LEAD a poisonous metal used by the Romans for making cosmetics and water pipes.

LIQUAMEN a very popular, strong-tasting sauce made of fermented fish. It was probably useful for hiding the taste of meat or fish which was not very fresh.

LUDI games put on and paid for by the Emperor or any wealthy citizen. They included chariot racing, gladiator fights and plays. (Singular: *ludus*).

MAGISTRATE a holder of high political office in Rome. Magistrates helped collect taxes and maintain law and order.

MOSAIC a wall or floor decoration made of broken pieces of tile or glass set in plaster.

PATERFAMILIAS the head of a household; the father of the family.

PATRON the head of a family which offered a client protection in return for political loyalty.

PROVINCE an area outside Rome which the Romans had conquered and now ruled. The rest of Italy was considered to be a province of Rome.

RHETORIC the art of speaking well in public so that you persuade your audience to think as you do.

SENATOR a member of the Senate, the council which ruled Rome during the Republic. The Senate survived into the imperial period (after Augustus took power) but its powers were much reduced.

STRIGIL a metal instrument for scraping oil, sweat and dirt off the body.

THERMAE the public baths.

THERMOPOLIUM a fast food shop where poorer Romans could buy hot meals.

VILLA a large country house and the farmland surrounding it. Many villa owners also had houses in town.

Page numbers in bold refer to illustrations

A

abacus **26**
actors **31**
aedile **31**, **32**
Aesculapius 25, **25**
amphitheatres 16, 47
amphora **17**, **21**, **34**, 47
aqueducts 16, **17**, 43, 47
aquila **36**, 47
arches, triumphal 16, **17**
army 6, **19**, 28, **32**, 33, **33**, 34, 36-37, **36-37**, **43**
Assembly 32, **32**
Augustus, Emperor 6, **29**, 32, 33, **39**, 42
auxiliaries 6, 39

B

babies **16**, **17**, **40**
bakers **17**, 21
basilica 16, **16**, 47
baths and bathhouses 16, **16**, **19**, 24, **24-25**
betrothal 40, **40**
books 27, **27**
boys 6, **18**, 22, 26, **26**, **27**, 40
bread 7, **17**, 20, 21, **21**, 36, **36**
bridges **16-17**
Britain (*Britannia*) 35, **36**
bulla **26**, **40**, 47

C

Caligula, Emperor 32, **33**
Capitol, the **26**
Caracalla, Baths of **24-25**
careers 27, 28-29
Carthage 35
carts 16, **34**
centuries (army units) 36
chariot racing 30, **30**, 31

cheese 20, 21
childbirth **18**, 27
children **18**, **25**, **37**; *see also* boys, girls
Christians and Christianity 6, 31
Circus Maximus 31, 47
cities 7, 14, 16, 24, 27, 33
citizens and citizenship 6, 18, **19**, 22, 32, **33**, 36, **37**, **42**, 47
clients 14, **18**, 19, 47
clothes 6, 7, **18**, 22, **22-23**, 24, **27**, **36**
Colosseum, the **31**
consuls 18, 32, 47
cooking 14, **18**, **20**, 21, **27**
craftsmen 28, **28**, 29, **29**
cremation 41
crops 7, 17

D

Dacia (Rumania) **19**
death **37**, 40, 41
dinner parties 20-21
Diocletian, Emperor, **33**, 42
divorce 40
doctors 7, 25, **25**, 28
domus 15, 47
dowry 40, **40**

E

education 26-27, **26**, 27
Egypt 20, **23**, 35, **39**
Empire, the Roman 6, 7, 18, 19, 28, 34, 36, 42
entertainment 30-31, **30-31**
equites **18**, **19**

F

families 7, 14, 15, 18-**19**, **37**, 40
farms and farming 7, 15, **17**, 37
fire 14, **33**
fish 20, **20**, 21
flats (*insulae*) 14, **14**, 16, 47

food 7, 20-21, **30**, **36**; *see also* meals
foodstalls 19, 21, **21**
forts **36**, **37**, 43
fortune tellers *see* soothsayers
forum **16**, **18**, 43, 47
France (*Gaul*) **19**, 35
frescoes 15, **43**, 47
fuller 24, **29**, 47
funerals 41, **41**
furniture 15, **29**

G

games (*ludi*) 30-31, **30-31**, 39, 47
Gaul *see* France
Germany (*Germania*) 35
girls 18, 26, **26**, **27**, 40, **40**
gladiators 30, **30**, 31, **31**
gods, family 6, **18**, **26**, 38, **38**, **40**
  Greek 38, 39
  state 6, 16, 25, **26**, **27**, 38-39, **38**-**39**
grain 7, 20; *see also* wheat
grapes 7, **17**, 21
Greece 35
Greek language, 7, 26, **26**
  people **19**, 26, **26**, 27, 28, 31

H

Hades 41
Hadrian, Emperor 33, **33**, 43
Hadrian's Wall 35, **36**
hair 18, 22, **22**, **23**, 27
haruspex 38
health **24**
heating 14, **15**
Hedone **19**, **42**
herbs 25, **25**
Hispania see Spain
holidays 30, 39, 40
hospital 35, 37
household gods *see* family gods
houses and homes 7, 14-15, **14-15**, 33

I, J

illness 25

Jesus Christ 33
jewellery **18**, 22, **22**
Judaea **19**, 33
judges 32, 33
Julius Caesar 6

L

lamps 15, **29**, 31
lararium 38, 47
lares 38, **38**
Latin 7, 26, **26**, **27**, 31, 42, **42**
law, the 27, 28, 32, 33
law courts 16, **32**, 33
legionary 6, 36, **36**
libraries 25, 27, 27
lictors 15
liquamen (fish sauce) 21, 47
ludi see games

M

magistrates **18**, **28**, 47
make-up 18, 22, **22**
marriage 27, **37**, 40, **40-41**
meals 18, **19**, 20-21
meat 20, **21**
merchants 32, 35
money 35, **37**, 42, **42**
mosaics 14, 15, 20, **43**, 47
mule 34
  Marius's 37
musical instruments **30**, **39**, 41

N

Naples 42, 43
nobiles 18, **18**
numbers 7, **26**

O

olive oil 7, 15, 17, 20, **21**, 24, 35, **35**
olives 7, 17, 20, **21**
operations 25, **25**
Ostia 14, 35

P

Pantheon, the **42-43**
Pax Romana 6, 34
penates 38, **38**
plebeians 18, **19**
politics 18, 27, 28, **32**
Pompeii 14, 15, 21, **42-43**
pottery **29**
praetor 32
prayers 18, **38**
priest 38, **39**
priestess **26**, 28, **39**
prisoners of war 7, **29**, 36
provinces 6, 18, **32**, 34, 39, **42**, 47
public speaking **26**, 27, **35**, 47
punishments **33**

Q

quaestor 32

R

religion 6, 16, **18**, **26**, **27**, 38-39
Remus 16
Republic, the Roman 6, 32
rhetoric *see* public speaking
Rhine, river **36**, 37
roads 6, 34, **34**, 36, 43
Rome, city of 6, 7, **14**, 16, **16-17**, 27, 28, 29, 31, 32, 35, 42
Romulus 16

S

sacrifices 6, 38, **38**, **39**
sandals **18**, **23**, 28, **37**
Saturnalia **39**
school **26**, **27**
Senate, the 6, 19, 32, **33**
senators 6, **23**, **28**, 32, **32**, 47
ships **16-17**, 34-35
shops 14, **16**, 21, 28, 29, **29**
Sibyll, the **39**

slaves 7, 14, 15, **17**, 18, **18**, 19, **19**, **20**, 21, **21**, 22, 24, **26**, 27, **28**, **29**, **36**, 39, **42**
soldiers 36-37, **36-37**, 39; *see also* army
soothsayers 6, **35**
Spain (*Hispania*) 35, **35**
strigil 24
superstitions 6, **38**

T

taxes 28, 32
teachers 7, **26**, 28
temples 6, 16, **16**, 25, **26**, **27**, 38, **42-43**
testudo (tortoise) **36**, **37**
theatre 16, 30, 31, **31**
Tiber, river 6, **16-17**
toga 6, 22, **23**, 24
  praetexta 6
  virilis 6, 22, 26
toilets **24**
tombs 41, 42
towns 16, 24, **42-43**
trade 6, 34-35
transport 34, 35

V

Vestal Virgin 27, 28, **39**
villa 14, 15, **43**, 47

W

wagons 34, **36**, 37, **37**
war 38, **39**
water 14, 16, 20, 21, **21**
weapons 36, **36**, 37, **37**
weaving 27
wedding **40-41**; *see also* marriage
wheat 35
wigs **22**, **23**
wild animals 30, **31**, 35
wine 7, 17, **17**, 20, **20**, 21, 25, 35, **36**, **39**
women 6, **18**, 21, 22, **22**, **28**, 30, 31, 40, **40-41**
writing 7, 26, **26**

ANSWERS

HAVE YOU SURVIVED?

Here are the quiz answers, with pages to turn to if you need an explanation.

Q

1 (B) - page 38
2 (C) - page 24
3 (B) - page 30
4 (A) - pages 26 & 40
5 (C) - page 16
6 (A) - page 24
7 (C) - page 36

8 (B) - pages 8 & 26
9 (B) - pages 16
10 (A) - page 22
11 (C) - page 35
12 (A) - page 27
13 (C) - page 21
14 (B) - page 29

Count up your correct answers and find out what your survival rating is.

13 - 14 Excellent! Just the sort of citizen the Emperor is looking for.
10 - 12 A top job in the provinces may be in the pipeline for you.
6 - 9   Not very impressive but, as a Roman would say, *Nil desperandum* (Do not despair)!
5 - 0   Awful! You might find yourself next on the programme at the Colosseum!

ACKNOWLEDGEMENTS

The Salariya Book Co Ltd would like to thank the following people for their assistance:

Sarah Ridley

John Wrighton